My PRAIRIE

COOKBOOK

My PRAIRIE

COOKBOOK

Memories and Frontier Food from
My Little House to Yours

———⟡———

MELISSA GILBERT

Photographs by Dane Holweger
Photography Direction and
Styling by Karen Schaupeter

STEWART, TABORI & CHANG
NEW YORK

Published in 2014 by Stewart, Tabori & Chang
An imprint of ABRAMS

Library of Congress Control Number: 2014930939

ISBN: 978-1-4197-0778-0

Editor: Holly Dolce and Jennifer Levesque
Designer: Chin-Yee Lai
Production Manager: Anet Sirna-Bruder

The text of this book was composed in New Baskerville and Trade Gothic.

Printed and bound in the United States

10 9 8 7 6 5 4 3 2 1

Stewart, Tabori & Chang books are available at special discounts when purchased
in quantity for premiums and promotions as well as fundraising or educational use.
Special editions can also be created to specification. For details, contact
specialsales@abramsbooks.com or the address below.

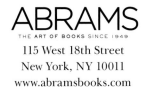

ABRAMS
THE ART OF BOOKS SINCE 1949
115 West 18th Street
New York, NY 10011
www.abramsbooks.com

For

TIMMY

In sickness and in health,

In plenty and in poverty,

In life and beyond,

Where we shall meet,
remember, and love again.

CONTENTS

MAIN COURSES

SIDES

DESSERTS

Introduction

Little House on the Prairie. Just saying those words evokes in fans a comforting nostalgia and a sense of family. And, yes, even love. For me, *Little House on the Prairie* means "home" in the truest sense of the word. That's where I grew up. I often tell people that I grew up in the seventies—the 1870s!

I was Laura. Laura was Melissa. We were melded together. I hunted frogs, fished, rode my horse, played with Jack the dog—all *off* camera. I did the same on camera, but off camera was even more fun. Don't get me wrong—the work part was fantastic, but it was also serious business. For me, at the tender ages of nine through nineteen, to be taken seriously and to help collaborate on the making of that show was a great gift. I felt respected and trusted. I felt capable. I felt special. *Little House on the Prairie* shaped me into the person I am today. Not only did I learn life lessons from behind the scenes, I also learned them from the material we were filming.

People are always asking me questions about those wonderful *Little House* days—in fact, you'll find many answers to FAQs in the pages that follow—but one of the things I'm asked about most often is the food. Food was such a big part of the show, and the questions range from "What did they really eat back in those days?" to "What did they serve at Nellie's restaurant?" to "What were you really eating when you filmed the dinner scenes?" (The surprising answer: It was often Kentucky Fried Chicken!) Because there is such interest in this subject, I started thinking a lot about prairie food and my own recipes. I have a large family (and there are a lot of men in it), and they love nothing more than when I make a big, comforting meal that they can dig into. So included in this cookbook are all the prairie classics: fried chicken, baked ham, corn bread, apple pie, and many more. When I can, I try to put a healthy spin on the dishes, for our modern lifestyles, as in the Very Veggie Soup (page 52) and the Greeny McGreen Green Salad (page 142). I've also included recipes for some of my long-time personal family favorites—such as Puffy Oven Pancake (page 22) and My Tuna-Noodle Casserole (page 78). Some of these family favorites would fit right into the prairie world, while others are more contemporary in their ingredients or preparation. I love nothing more than to see my family truly enjoy a meal I've prepared. It fills up my mom/wife heart. I hope these recipes will do the same things for you and the people you love.

Aside from these nearly eighty simple and delicious dishes, I've also included lots of stories, anecdotes, and images that show and tell what it was like behind the scenes of our show. I've tried to answer all of the questions from fans and tell them the things they've wanted to know. So, aside from a scrumptious collection of my favorite recipes and some insanely beautiful photos of them, you'll also be able to peek behind the scenes of *Little House*, which was such a significant part of my life for so many years.

Fans of the show tell me how *Little House* made them strive for all that really matters in life: family, love, community, faith, respect, and tolerance. I am a fan, too, and I think that a large part of the appeal of the show is because it has always grounded us. Each episode has a lesson, a message. Life gets rough. There is a lot of turmoil in the world. Times change. Technology changes, but *Little House on the Prairie* lives on because the stories are simple. Love thy neighbor. Do unto others as you would have them do unto you. Believe in yourself and others. And, maybe even the most important, prepare a delightful family dinner that everyone can sit down to together at the end of a long day and share. Some people might describe these ideals as simplistic, but I think it's the opposite. It is easier to be cynical, closed off, and angry. It is much harder to be open, loving, kind, and generous of spirit.

Little House fans know this. That is why they are so loyal and constant. All over the world, people watch our show because they want to be reminded of what it's like to feel. *Little House on the Prairie* opens people's hearts. It definitely opened mine.

I miss my *Prairie* family and think of them every day. Especially my Pa. This one's for you, Mike. I do hope I've made you proud.

Love,

Half-Pint

Breakfast

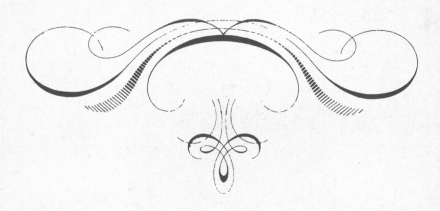

LITTLE HOUSE:
THE EARLY YEARS

Little House on the Prairie began on the NBC network on September 11, 1974, and ended on May 10, 1982. During the 1982–83 television season, it was broadcast with a new title, *Little House: A New Beginning*. Michael Landon was the star and executive producer of the show and also directed the largest number of episodes—eighty-seven! And I was Laura (lucky girl).

How do I even find the words to describe what the early years of filming *Little House on the Prairie* were like? It was fun. Pure, unadulterated fun! Every day was a new adventure for me, playing dress-up in prairie clothes and working with such a warm and talented cast and crew. We quickly became a family.

The crew was very close. Some of them had worked together for decades—and a few of them had worked with Mike on *Bonanza*. Michael Landon was our boss, our father, and our mentor. Kent McCray was his co–executive producer, sergeant at arms, and best friend. Together they created an atmosphere of loyalty and the best kind of creativity. They also allowed us to have fun while we were working. Actually, Mike didn't just allow fun—he rather insisted on it.

From my very first day on the set, I felt that I was part of something very special. Working on the *Little House* set was a dream come true for an adventurous little girl like me. There were other kids to play with and also dogs, horses, cows, chickens, wolves, and rabbits—all of them were tratined and there for me to play with. And play I did. In many ways, it didn't feel like work. I suppose that's the way it should be for a child in my business. Though I could and would hunker down and be serious in a heavy scene, I remember the early years as being more fun than I could have dreamed.

I also remember watching the adults around me in absolute awe. I was thunderstruck by Karen Grassle (Caroline). She was so beautiful and different—earthier than any woman I had known before. She was very well trained as an actor and had a grace that drew me to her. I'd watch her breathe and the way she moved her hands. She was the personification of beauty. And Victor French (Isaiah) could make me laugh until my sides hurt. He could also make me cry by looking at me just the right way.

I didn't fully know it at the time, but I was surrounded by some of the most talented actors in the business. I was also lucky to be surrounded by an incredibly talented crew. They all did their very difficult jobs so well that they made it look easy. They spoiled me forever. To this day, I am totally perplexed when a crew doesn't work well together. I am also perplexed when a work environment isn't fun. Hey, I learned from the best, so I have very high expectations!

One of our first TV Guide shoots. Anytime we did still photos, Mike would make us laugh. Looks like it was my turn to make us laugh this time.

Oh how I adored Victor French!!

ERNIE BORGNINE (LEFT) AND MELISSA GILBERT NBC-TV'S "LITTLE HOUSE ON THE PRAIRIE" WEDNESDAY, DEC. 18, 1974   11/19/74

That's Uncle Miles. He was one of our first assistant directors. Behind him is Ted Voightlander. He was one of our cinematographers.

Melissa Gilbert

in her continuing role as Laura Ingalls
in

"LITTLE HOUSE ON THE PRAIRIE"
From the Book by Laura Ingalls Wilder
TONIGHT.   8 P.M.   NBC-TV

Public Relations: Freeman & Doff   XXXX   Personal Mgt.: Ron Samuels

IT ALL
STARTED
HERE

These are all pictures from behind the scenes of the filming of the pilot movie in 1973.

The man putting makeup on my wee little face is Whitey Snyder. He was Marilyn Monroe's personal makeup artist!

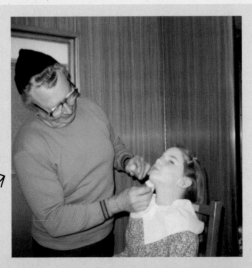

PUFFY OVEN PANCAKE

This dish is a variation on the classic baked pancake theme. I found that when my whole family was at home, it was really hard to serve them piping-hot griddle pancakes all at the same time. So I started playing around with recipes that could be baked in the oven. This is my own version of what some people call a "Dutch baby." That seems like a really gruesome name to me—*puffy pancake* sounds so much more appetizing. I prefer mine with just a touch of powdered sugar. Feel free to serve yours with your favorite syrup, jelly, or fruit. In fact, you can put all the toppings on the table and let everyone create their own breakfast treat.

 Serves 6

5 tablespoons (70 g) unsalted
   butter
1½ cups (180 g) all-purpose flour
6 large eggs
1½ cups (360 ml) milk
Warm maple syrup, for serving
Chopped fresh fruit, for serving

- Preheat the oven to 400°F (205°C).

- Put the butter in a 9-by-13-inch (23-by-33-cm) glass baking dish and place it in the oven for a few minutes to let the butter melt. Carefully tilt the dish so that the bottom and sides are coated with the butter.

- Whisk together the flour, eggs, and milk in a large bowl. Pour the batter into the dish. Bake for 20 minutes, or until golden and puffy.

- Serve with the syrup and fruit.

FRENCH BREAD FRENCH TOAST

French toast is an all-around favorite here at my house. I've made many variations over the years, but this one, with sturdy, super thick–cut French bread, is the biggest hit. I love that I can please everyone's palate with the choice of topping. I put sliced strawberries, blueberries, sliced bananas, assorted jams, jellies, maple syrup, boysenberry syrup, melted butter, and confectioners' sugar on the table (same as the puffy pancake, opposite). You want to know how I know my family loves it? There is absolute silence at the table for at least 15 minutes!

Serves 4 to 6

- Whisk the eggs, milk, sugar, cinnamon, nutmeg, and vanilla in a large bowl. Pour them into a 9-by-13-inch (23-by-33-cm) baking dish. Add the bread slices and soak the bread in the egg mixture for about 5 minutes on each side (the bread should absorb all of the liquid).

- Melt the butter in a large skillet over medium heat, and cook the bread in batches until golden on both sides, 3 to 4 minutes per side.

- Serve immediately, sprinkled with confectioners' sugar.

6 large eggs
¼ cup (60 ml) milk
1 teaspoon granulated sugar
1 teaspoon ground cinnamon
¼ teaspoon ground nutmeg
Dash of vanilla extract
1 large loaf crusty French bread, cut into 1- to 1½-inch (2.5- to 4-cm) slices
2 tablespoons unsalted butter
Confectioners' sugar, for serving

HOMEMADE SAUSAGE WITH APPLES

I always loved shooting breakfast scenes on *Little House*. The whole soundstage would smell of sausage, bacon, eggs, biscuits, and whatever else we were eating in the scene. There was often plenty left over, so when the scenes were over, I would eat and eat and eat. Breakfast sausage has always been one of my favorite choices, so I started playing around with a recipe for homemade sausage and started pairing it with various flavors. The combination of the smokiness of the pork sausage patties with the sweetness of the apples makes a great energizing start to a busy day. Or it can be served as part of a larger spread with eggs and biscuits—or serve it with my French toast (page 23). It's also the perfect beginning to a cozy stay-in-your-jammies Sunday.

Serves 4 to 6

- Mix the pork, sage, salt, nutmeg, black pepper, and cayenne (if using) in a large bowl. Form into 8 patties.

- Fry the patties in a large skillet until golden brown on both sides, 5 to 8 minutes per side. Drain on paper towels.

- Cook the apples in the same skillet in the sausage drippings, turning them over until they are evenly browned, 5 to 7 minutes. Sprinkle the sugar and cinnamon over the apples and cook for a few minutes longer, until they are glazed.

- Return the sausage to the skillet to warm it before serving with the apples.

2 pounds (910 g) ground pork shoulder
2 tablespoons chopped fresh sage leaves
1 tablespoon salt
1 teaspoon ground nutmeg
Freshly ground black pepper
Pinch of cayenne pepper (optional)
3 Pippin or other firm, tart apples, peeled, cored, and cut into wedges
1 tablespoon granulated sugar
1 tablespoon ground cinnamon

STOVETOP BISCUITS WITH SAUSAGE GRAVY

Now *this* is prairie food. I've actually eaten biscuits and gravy from an authentic chuck wagon. I'd eat biscuits and gravy anytime, anywhere. Though if I did eat biscuits and gravy as often as I'd like, my rear end would be as wide as the prairie itself. I've included a recipe for from-scratch biscuits here, but true confession: I love the recipe from the Bisquick box. Serve this with fried eggs, if you like.

Serves 8 to 10 in a normal home, but 4 to 6 with my dudes

12 ounces (340 g) hot bulk sausage

12 ounces (340 g) mild bulk sausage

¼ cup (30 g) all-purpose flour

2 quarts (2 L) milk

Salt and freshly ground black pepper

Stovetop Biscuits (recipe opposite)

- Put both kinds of sausage in a large pot and cook over medium heat until browned and cooked through, 8 to 10 minutes. Drain the fat, and then add the flour to the sausage. Raise the heat to medium-high and cook until the sausage is well coated with the flour. Add the milk and cook, stirring, for 20 to 25 minutes, or until it reaches the desired thickness.

- Season with salt and pepper to taste. Serve over the biscuits.

- Whisk together the flour, baking powder, and salt in a large bowl. Add the lard and rub it in with your fingers until the mixture is mealy. Add the milk and mix until a smooth dough forms. Divide the dough in half, and form each half into 6 balls. Flatten each ball to be about ¼ inch (6 mm) thick.

- Melt a tablespoon or two of lard in a medium cast-iron skillet over medium-low heat. Add 6 dough pieces and fry on both sides until browned, about 6 minutes per side. Drain on paper towels and repeat with the remaining dough pieces.

Makes 12 biscuits

2 cups (250 g) all-purpose flour
4 teaspoons baking powder
1 teaspoon salt
¼ cup (50 g) cold lard or vegetable shortening, cut into bits, plus more for the skillet
1 cup (240 ml) milk

CRISPY HOME FRIES

This recipe is so yummy and really easy. It's a great basic technique to master, and you can dress it up any way you want. Add fried eggs and your favorite shredded cheese on top, or sprinkle with chopped smoked trout and sour cream. You can mince some bell pepper or cooked chopped bacon and add it to the onion layer while cooking. You could even serve these home fries for dinner with a steak and gravy on top. Be creative and have fun, and your family will thank you.

 *Serves 2 to 4*

3 tablespoons grapeseed, canola, or peanut oil
2 large russet potatoes, peeled and thinly sliced (about ⅛ inch/ 3 mm thick)
1 medium yellow onion, thinly sliced
Salt and freshly ground black pepper

- Heat 2 tablespoons of the oil in a large skillet on medium-high heat until sizzling. Place a single layer of potato slices on the bottom of the pan. Add a light layer of sliced onions. Sprinkle with salt and pepper. Add another layer of potatoes, another layer of onion slices, and sprinkle again with salt and pepper. Keep layering until you've used up your potatoes and onions.

- Lower the heat to medium and cover the skillet. Let it cook undisturbed for about 10 minutes, until the potato layer at the bottom is nicely browned. You can move it aside a little bit with a spatula to see if the bottom edges are browned.

- Gently flip the potatoes over, a section of the pan at a time, so that the layer that was on the top is now on the bottom and the browned potatoes are now on top. (Or, if you're feeling daring, invert a dinner plate over the skillet and flip the whole thing over, then slide the potato cake back into the skillet.) Add the remaining 1 tablespoon oil, coaxing it to the bottom of the skillet. Cover and let it cook for another 5 to 10 minutes, until the bottom layer is browned.

- Remove the lid and continue to cook for 5 more minutes. Slide the potatoes onto a platter and cut it into servings. Serve immediately.

SAUSAGE AND EGG BREAKFAST CASSEROLE

I start this hearty country dish on Christmas Eve to serve on Christmas morning. It's a family tradition as well as a family favorite. There's usually an army at my house—my boys, their women, my husband's kids, and their significant others. But this is especially great for a company breakfast any time of year. You can cut this recipe in half if you have fewer than the twelve mouths that I have to feed.

continued

3 pounds (1.4 kg) ground bulk
   breakfast sausage of your
   choice
18 large eggs
6 cups (1.4 L) milk
3 teaspoons dry mustard
2 teaspoons salt
8 slices white bread, torn into
   pieces
1 cup (4 ounces/115 g) grated
   cheese (I like sharp Cheddar
   and Monterey Jack, or pepper
   Jack for a little extra spice)

- Brown the sausage well in a large skillet over medium heat. Drain thoroughly.

- Beat the eggs, milk, mustard, and salt together in a very large bowl. Add the bread, cheese, and sausage and mix to combine. Pour the mixture into two 9-by-13-inch (23-by-33-cm) glass baking dishes. Cover and refrigerate overnight.

- Remove the baking dishes from the refrigerator to take the chill off and preheat the oven to 350°F (175°C). Bake the casseroles for about 50 minutes, until firm throughout and browned on top. Serve hot.

AMANDA'S CHUNKY EGGS

My friend Amanda is one of the funniest and most creative people I know. We've been friends since I met her on the set of *Touched by an Angel*. She is also the fittest person I know. Her philosophy—and mine—is to eat foods as they are intended. For example, sugar instead of artificial sweetener, nothing reduced fat, no chemical alterations, nothing genetically modified. Just eat in moderation. Amanda, whom I've nicknamed Fancy Hands because she is a remarkable massage therapist, made these eggs for me the day before I opened in the *Little House* musical a few years back. Now, I don't drink alcohol, but Amanda insists that I tell you to "Enjoy with a Bellini!"

Serves 4

- Beat the eggs and milk into submission in a large bowl.

- Heat the butter in a large skillet over medium-low heat. Add the egg mixture and cook, stirring. As it begins to set, add half of the cheese and continue to cook and stir. Remove from the heat when the eggs are fluffy but not dry.

- Add the remaining cheese to the hot eggs and quickly stir for a moment. Place 1 or 2 slices of tomato on each plate and top with the chunky eggs. Season with salt and pepper to taste.

8 large eggs
1 cup (240 ml) milk
2 tablespoons unsalted butter
1 wedge Brie cheese (6 to 8 ounces/170 to 225 g), cut into chunks
1 large ripe heirloom tomato (one of those big ugly ones), sliced
Salt and freshly ground black pepper

KELLY'S CREAMY EGGS

This recipe is one of my favorite breakfast recipes of all time. It's great for a big crowd. I first had it when visiting my friend Brian Wimmer in Sundance, Utah. A whole bunch of us, about ten adults and about twenty kids, got together at our friend Kelly Warnick's place in Wales, Utah. We all went out for pizza and to a drive-in movie and we all stayed over, some in the house, some in the tree house, some in tents, and I slept in the back of Kelly's vintage pickup truck.

The next morning, we were all starving, and Kelly served us these eggs, which are so rich and warm and yummy, and so simple. Kids love them, and so do adults!

 *Serves 6 to 12*

3 cups (720 ml) heavy whipping cream
12 large eggs
Salt and freshly ground black pepper
Toasted bread, for serving

- Preheat the oven to 375°F (190°C).

- Pour the cream into a 9-by-13-inch (23-by-33-cm) glass baking dish. Crack the eggs directly into the dish, spacing them out evenly in the cream. Season liberally with salt and pepper. Feel free to get fancy here. Use garlic salt or even yummier truffle salt.

- Bake for 45 to 60 minutes. Serve hot over toast.

SPICY PUMPKIN MUFFINS

I especially love to make these muffins a couple of weeks before Thanksgiving. They get everyone in the winter holiday mood. I serve these warm with cream cheese to spread on them. I usually leave out the golden raisins, but they do make a lovely addition if you like raisins.

Makes 24 muffins

- Preheat the oven to 400°F (205°C). Grease and flour two standard 12-cup muffin pans.

- Mix together in a food processor (or use a handheld electric mixer) the flour, brown sugar, granulated sugar, baking soda, cinnamon, nutmeg, and salt. Add the butter and blend until it resembles coarse meal. Add the raisins, buttermilk, pumpkin puree, and eggs, and mix until moist.

- Divide the batter among the prepared muffin cups, filling them three-quarters full. Bake for 18 minutes, or until lightly browned on top. Remove them to a wire rack to cool.

2 cups (250 g) self-rising flour
¾ cup (165 g) firmly packed light brown sugar
¼ cup (50 g) granulated sugar
1 teaspoon baking soda
1 teaspoon ground cinnamon
1 teaspoon ground nutmeg
½ teaspoon salt
½ cup (1 stick/115 g) unsalted butter, softened
1 cup (145 g) golden raisins
¾ cup (180 ml) buttermilk
1 (15-ounce/425-g) can pumpkin puree (not pumpkin pie filling)
2 large eggs, lightly beaten

BIG OL' BLUEBERRY MUFFINS

So easy, and your family will be so excited to wake up to these blueberry-studded muffins. Nothing gets teenagers out of bed faster than the smell of baking in the morning. To you, it will smell like Victory.

Makes 12 muffins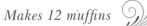

- Preheat the oven to 400°F (205°C). Grease and flour a standard 12-cup muffin pan.

- Mix the flour, sugar, baking powder, and salt in a large bowl. Combine the eggs and oil in a small bowl, add the milk, and then stir into the dry ingredients until just moistened. Stir the blueberries into the mixture.

- Divide the batter among the prepared muffin cups, filling them halfway. Bake for 20 minutes, or until lightly golden on top. Remove them to a wire rack to cool.

3 cups (375 g) all-purpose flour
1 cup (200 g) granulated sugar
4 teaspoons baking powder
1 teaspoon salt
2 large eggs, lightly beaten
½ cup (120 ml) vegetable oil, plus extra for the pan
1 cup (240 ml) milk
1½ cups (255 g) blueberries (preferably fresh, but thawed frozen will work too)

SWEET-TART APPLE MUFFINS

There was a lot of apple fritter–making on *Little House*. Ma was always rolling dough for fritters. Now, I'm not knocking fritters, but I prefer not to send my kids off to school completely overloaded with sugar. So I turned those apple fritters into muffins. There's still sugar, but not quite as much. I think Ma would be proud, don't you?

 *Makes 12 muffins*

1½ cups (180 g) all-purpose flour
½ cup (100 g) granulated sugar
2 teaspoons baking powder
½ teaspoon salt
1 teaspoon ground cinnamon
¼ cup (50 g) vegetable shortening
1 large egg
½ cup (120 ml) milk
1 cup (130 g) finely chopped
apples (I like to mix sweet and tart varieties)
⅓ cup (65 g) firmly packed light brown sugar
⅓ cup (40 g) chopped walnuts

- Preheat the oven to 400°F (205°C). Grease and flour a standard 12-cup muffin pan.

- Mix the flour, sugar, baking powder, salt, and ½ teaspoon of the cinnamon in a large bowl. Blend the shortening, egg, milk, and apples in another bowl. Add to the dry ingredients and stir until thoroughly blended.

- Divide the batter among the prepared muffin cups, filling them three-quarters full. Top with the brown sugar, nuts, and the remaining ½ teaspoon of the cinnamon. Bake for 25 to 30 minutes, until lightly golden on top. Remove them to a wire rack to cool.

PRAIRIE CHRISTMAS GINGERBREAD

I fell in love with gingerbread on the set of *Little House*. Every Christmas episode we shot, there would be gingerbread somewhere on the set, either right in a scene we were doing, or one of the women from the crew or maybe one of the kids' moms would make it for snacking. I would sneak little bites, hoping that no one would notice. But they noticed all right, particularly when the entire loaf of gingerbread was gone. Across the soundstage I'd hear someone call, "Half-Pint! Where's the gingerbread?" Then, inevitably, I'd be caught and tickled into promising never to do it again.

I broke that promise more times than I can count. Gingerbread and tickles? What kid wouldn't break a promise if that were the result?

Serves 9

- Preheat the oven to 350°F (175°C). Grease and flour an 8-inch (20-cm) square baking pan.

- Combine the flour, brown sugar, cinnamon, ginger, baking powder, and baking soda in a large bowl. Add the shortening, molasses, egg, and ½ cup (120 ml) water. Beat with an electric mixer on low to medium speed until combined, then beat on high speed for 2 minutes.

- Pour the batter into the prepared baking pan. Bake for 35 to 40 minutes or until a toothpick inserted near the center comes out clean. Cool on a rack for 10 minutes, then invert the pan to remove the gingerbread.

1½ cups (180 g) all-purpose flour
¼ cup (55 g) firmly packed light brown sugar
¾ teaspoon ground cinnamon
¾ teaspoon ground ginger
½ teaspoon baking powder
½ teaspoon baking soda
½ cup (100 g) vegetable shortening
½ cup (120 ml) light molasses
1 large egg

FIG-DATE-NUT BREAD

———————⟨⟨◆◇◆⟩⟩———————

Nearly every Sunday when I was a little girl, my grandfather would take me to Du-par's coffee shop for breakfast. After my delicious meal, my grandpa would send me home with a loaf of date-nut bread. I always picked the nuts out, then ate my bread with cream cheese on it. It was one of my all-time favorite treats. Here is my version of the recipe. I've included the nuts for the sake of tradition, but I always omit them when I make this; I'm just not a nut fan.

Makes one 8½-inch (21.5-cm) loaf

- Combine the dates, figs, butter, and baking soda in a large bowl. Pour in the boiling water, stir well, and let stand for 15 minutes.

- Preheat the oven to 350°F (175°C). Grease and flour an 8½-inch (21.5-cm) loaf pan.

- With an electric mixer, beat the sugar, walnuts, and eggs into the date mixture. In a medium bowl, stir and toss together the all-purpose and whole-wheat flours, the baking powder, and salt. Add to the date mixture and beat just until blended.

- Spread the batter evenly in the prepared pan. Bake until a thin wooden skewer inserted in the center of the loaf comes out clean, 55 to 65 minutes. Cool in the pan for 10 minutes, then turn it out onto a wire rack to cool completely.

Hint: For a yummy snack or treat, slice and toast the bread, and then put butter or cream cheese on it. Your tongue will jump out of your mouth and slap you on the back of your head.

1 cup (170 g) chopped pitted dates
1 cup (170 g) chopped dried figs
¼ cup (½ stick/55 g) unsalted butter, softened
1½ teaspoons baking soda
1 cup (240 ml) boiling water
½ cup (100 g) granulated sugar
½ cup (55 g) chopped walnuts
2 large eggs
¾ cup (90 g) all-purpose flour
¾ cup (90 g) whole-wheat flour
½ teaspoon baking powder
½ teaspoon salt

TOO-GOOD-TO-BE-TRUE MULTIGRAIN BREAD

⟴

I have to be honest—I was always more of a Wonder Bread girl. Then, once, I was on location in northern Oregon, shooting a movie, and I went into this little café for breakfast. They served me the most amazing multigrain bread I'd ever tasted. They wouldn't give me their recipe, so I came home and started trying to create one of my own. It only took me twenty years, but here it is! It's so easy you will hardly believe it. You can use any textured grain, small seeds, and so forth for the oats, so long as it's something that does not require par-cooking before use. Try this free-form loaf with some simple homemade jam for a lighter prairie-style breakfast.

 Makes 2 approximately 1-pound (455-g) loaves

4 cups (500 g) all-purpose flour
1 cup (125 g) whole-wheat flour
1 cup (100 g) rye flour
½ cup (about 80 g) steel-cut oats, stone-ground cornmeal, hulled sunflower seeds, flaxseeds, sesame seeds, or finely chopped almonds
1 tablespoon kosher salt
½ teaspoon instant yeast
Strawberry Jam (recipe opposite), for serving

- Mix together all three flours, the oats, salt, and yeast in a very large bowl. Stir in 3¼ cups (780 ml) room-temperature water to form a very thick, sticky dough. Cover the bowl and let it sit at warm room temperature for 8 hours or overnight, until it doubles in size.

- When you're ready to shape and bake the loaves, sprinkle your work surface with a little flour. Turn the dough out onto the counter and divide it in half. Sprinkle the dough pieces with a little more flour and shape them into oblong loaves on a baking sheet. Cover and let the loaves rise for about 1½ hours at warm room temperature, or until nearly doubled in size.

- Meanwhile, preheat the oven to 450°F (230°C). Put a baking pan in the bottom of the oven to preheat as well.

- When the loaves have risen, quickly cut ½-inch (12-mm) slashes in the top with a knife and set the loaves in the oven. (Leave them on the baking sheet, or use a baking stone if you have one.) Pour ½ cup (120 ml) water into the pan at the bottom of the oven to create steam and close the oven door. Bake for 30 to 35 minutes, until the loaves are dark brown, sound hollow when tapped, and the inside registers 190°F (90°C) on an instant-read thermometer. Allow the loaves to cool fully on a wire rack.

STRAWBERRY JAM

- Put a small dish (like a saucer) in the freezer to chill. Combine the berries, sugar, and lemon juice in a large stainless-steel skillet over medium heat, stirring until the sugar dissolves. Raise the heat to medium-high and boil, stirring and skimming off the foam with a spoon for several minutes, until the mixture starts to look like thin jam. It's done when a small dollop firms up when dropped onto the frozen dish.

- Transfer the jam to clean glass jars and store in the refrigerator for up to 1 month.

Makes 2 pints (960 ml)

2 pounds (910 g) strawberries, hulled and lightly mashed
2 cups (400 g) granulated sugar
¼ cup (60 ml) freshly squeezed lemon juice

SOUPS

AND

STEWS

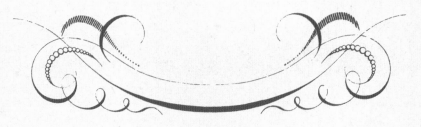

MY PA

I met Michael Landon in the winter of 1973. He was a huge TV star. I was a little kid from the San Fernando Valley. I had no idea who he was. All I knew was that my family was making an awfully big deal out of the fact that I was going to meet him.

When the moment came that I first walked into the casting office and saw him, I knew why everyone had made such a big deal about him. He was magnetic, warm, charming, and super funny. The moment I looked into his eyes, I felt safe. He was one of those people whose smile lights up their whole self. Not just their mouth. His smile went all the way to the top of his head. He also didn't talk to me like I was just a kid. He talked to me like I was his peer. He made me feel like he respected my ability as a professional, and that made me want to do even better, go even further in our scenes.

I didn't know it at the time, but that first moment with Mike would be one of the defining moments of my life. We struck up an instant friendship. I would even go so far as to call it a kinship. Whenever I was with him, I believed completely that I was his Half-Pint and he was my Pa.

Everything I know and honor about being a professional in my industry, I learned from him. Mike was an extraordinary filmmaker. He had this amazing ability to envision a story that would move millions of people, and then put his pen to paper, write it, and mold it into grade-A entertainment—all the while infusing his work with messages about family, community, faith, and love.

Mike was a perfectionist. He did not suffer fools easily. He would give everyone a chance to learn, to step up and deliver. He nurtured everyone around him, but if they didn't deliver or fooled around too much or didn't know their lines or treated someone on his crew disrespectfully, they were gone. Those of us who worked within the parameters he set up for us as professionals found ourselves in the glow of his generous and loving praise. He really made us want to do well for him.

I also learned lessons from him about life, family, and love.

He worked crazy hours all the time, but I'd sometimes spend the night at his house because his kids were my closest friends—especially Leslie. He was very hands-on with us kids—watching scary movies with us, popping popcorn, and giving us crazy amounts of candy. His favorite—and mine—were jelly beans, especially the black ones. We'd save them up and share them with each other.

Mike had the greatest laugh you'd ever want to hear. It was infectious. When he laughed, I could see the boy that he once was. He was so full of mischief, and yet, when it was time to buckle down and do the work, he did it. And he did it brilliantly.

There really hasn't been another person like him in our business. Nor has there been another person like him in my life. I loved him. I loved him as a mentor, as a friend, and as my Pa. I always, always will.

My Father Is Michael Landon

AUGUST/SEPTEMBER 1976

JACK JILL

75c

TV Week

Return to 'Little House on the Prairie'

The Houston Post
Dec. 11-17

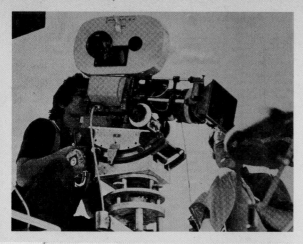

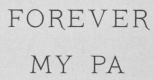

FOREVER
MY PA

VERY VEGGIE SOUP

For a long time, my kids didn't like anything that wasn't brown or white. I tried everything to get them to eat their veggies. Then I made this soup and they couldn't get enough. Maybe it's because I put a handful of tiny cubes of Muenster cheese in the bottom of their bowls and poured the soup over it. As the kids mixed it up, the melted cheese magically appeared. They got so excited! And I got some serious veggies into their bodies.

 *Serves 4*

---

2 tablespoons olive oil or unsalted butter
1 large yellow onion, coarsely chopped
1 cup (150 g) coarsely chopped baking potato
1 cup (130 g) coarsely chopped carrots
1 cup (90 g) coarsely chopped broccoli
1 cup (240 ml) vegetable broth
1 teaspoon dried oregano
1 teaspoon dried thyme
1 dried bay leaf
1 (15-ounce/425-g) can corn, drained
1 (16-ounce/455-g) package frozen green beans, thawed and drained
1 (15-ounce/425-g) can kidney beans, rinsed and drained
Salt and freshly ground black pepper

- In a large saucepan over medium heat, warm the oil or melt the butter. Add the onion and sauté until it begins to soften, 3 to 5 minutes.

- Add the potato, carrots, broccoli, broth, oregano, thyme, and bay leaf and bring them to a boil. Reduce the heat and simmer until the vegetables are tender, 15 to 20 minutes.

- Add the corn, green beans, and kidney beans and bring the soup back to a simmer; cook for 10 minutes. Discard the bay leaf, season to taste with salt and pepper, and serve hot.

BUTTERNUT SQUASH SOUP

There's really only one thing I can say about this smooth, flavorful, and nourishing soup: It's comfort in a bowl. Try it with the Too-Good-to-Be-True Multigrain Bread (page 42).

Serves 12 to 16

- Put the squash in a large pot, cover with 1 quart (960 ml) water, and add the salt; bring the water to a boil, then simmer on low until soft, about 40 minutes. Drain the squash, reserving 2 cups (480 ml) of the cooking liquid. Puree the squash with 1 cup (240 ml) of the reserved liquid and set aside.

- Melt half of the butter in a soup pot, add the wine, and sauté the celery, onion, and bell pepper for 5 minutes. Add the tarragon, cinnamon, nutmeg, and cloves. Add the broth and the remaining 1 cup (240 ml) reserved squash-cooking liquid. Bring to a boil.

- Meanwhile, melt the remaining butter in a small skillet, then sprinkle in the flour and cook, stirring constantly, until the roux is smooth and light brown.

- Thicken the soup by whisking in the roux. Add the pureed squash. Cook, stirring often, on low heat for 5 minutes. Add the maple syrup and sherry and mix well to combine and heat everything through. Serve hot.

2 pounds (910 g) butternut squash, peeled, seeded, and cut into large chunks
1 tablespoon salt
½ cup (1 stick/115 g) unsalted butter
¼ cup (60 ml) white wine
½ cup (50 g) diced celery
½ cup (60 g) diced yellow onion
½ cup (75 g) diced yellow bell pepper
1 teaspoon minced fresh tarragon leaves
½ teaspoon ground cinnamon
½ teaspoon ground nutmeg
½ teaspoon ground cloves
1 quart (960 ml) chicken broth
¼ cup (30 g) all-purpose flour
½ cup (120 ml) maple syrup
¼ cup (60 ml) dry sherry

POTATO AND SPRING ONION SOUP

This soup, which is great for really cold winter days, would have been a very easy one to prepare out on the prairie. In the winter, I will make a big pot of this soup in the late morning and just leave it on the stove until late afternoon. That way, anyone can grab a mugful at any time.

 Serves 4 to 6

2 bunches (about 10) spring onions, trimmed
¼ cup (60 ml) sunflower or vegetable oil
1 yellow onion, coarsely chopped
3 russet potatoes (about 1½ pounds/680 g), peeled and quartered
1 quart (960 ml) chicken broth
Salt and freshly ground black pepper

• Cut the spring onions in half crosswise, dividing the white and green parts. Coarsely chop the white parts and set aside. Finely chop the green parts and set them aside separately.

• Heat the oil in a medium pot over medium heat. Add the yellow onion and chopped white parts of the spring onions and cook, stirring often with a wooden spoon, until soft, 8 to 10 minutes. Add the potatoes and broth and season to taste with salt and pepper. Increase the heat to medium-high and bring just to a boil. Reduce the heat to medium-low and simmer, stirring occasionally, until the potatoes are soft, 30 to 35 minutes.

• Allow the soup to cool slightly. Working in batches, puree the soup in a blender or a food processor until very smooth. Return the pureed soup to the pot and cook over medium heat until hot. Adjust the seasonings to taste. Garnish individual servings with the reserved spring onion greens.

MUSHROOM-BARLEY SOUP

When I make this soup, I can picture Ma standing over her big black iron pot, wooden spoon in hand, welcoming Pa home from a long day working in the fields. This soup is hearty, restorative, and very, very prairie.

Serves 8

- Put the porcini mushrooms in a small bowl and add warm water to cover. Soak until softened, about 30 minutes.

- Line a strainer with a double layer of cheesecloth and set it inside a bowl. Pour the porcini and liquid into the strainer, reserving the liquid. Finely chop the porcini and set aside.

- In a large pot over medium heat, warm the oil and butter. Add the onion, celery, and carrot and sauté until the onion is translucent, 2 to 3 minutes. Add the button mushrooms, raise the heat to high, and sauté until the mushrooms begin to soften, 2 to 3 minutes more.

- Add the broth, barley, bay leaf, porcini, and reserved soaking liquid and bring them to a boil. Reduce the heat to low, cover partially, and simmer gently, stirring occasionally, until the barley is tender and the soup is thick, 50 to 60 minutes.

- Discard the bay leaf. Season to taste with salt and pepper. Garnish individual servings with the parsley.

½ ounce (15 g) dried porcini mushrooms (not so prairie, but so worth it)
2 tablespoons vegetable oil
2 tablespoons unsalted butter
1 yellow onion, finely chopped
1 celery stalk, finely chopped
1 carrot, finely chopped
8 ounces (225 g) fresh button mushrooms, thinly sliced
6 cups (1.4 L) beef or chicken broth
2 cups (400 g) pearl barley, rinsed under cold running water
1 dried bay leaf
Salt and freshly ground black pepper
¼ cup (7 g) finely chopped fresh parsley, for serving

MUSHROOM-BARLEY SOUP

MUSHROOM-BARLEY SOUP

GRANDMA BEETSIE'S
CHICKEN SOUP

CORN CHOWDER

CORN CHOWDER

I really love being able to make a big pot of hearty soup for dinner. It's a time-saver and the cleanup is always easier. This corn chowder is one of my family's favorites. The East and West Coasts have their seafood chowders, but we prairie folk raise a lot of corn. No prairie cookbook would be complete without a corn chowder recipe.

Serves 4

- Working over a large shallow bowl, slice the corn kernels off the cobs, scraping the cobs with the knife to extract the flavorful juices. Halve 5 of the bare corncobs crosswise, discarding the rest. Set the corn and cobs aside.

- Cook the bacon in a large pot over medium heat, stirring occasionally, until crisp, about 12 minutes. Reserve 3 tablespoons of the bacon for garnish, leaving the remaining bacon in the pot. Add the butter, garlic, celery, onion, thyme, and bay leaf. Cover the pot and cook, stirring occasionally, until the onion softens, about 6 minutes. Add the reserved corn kernels and cobs, the milk, and potatoes. Cover, bring to a boil, then reduce the heat to low and simmer, stirring occasionally, until the potatoes are tender, about 25 minutes.

- Skim any foam from the surface of the soup. Discard the cobs and bay leaf. Transfer 1½ cups (360 ml) of the soup to a blender and puree. Stir the puree back into the chowder to thicken it. Season with salt and pepper and serve garnished with the basil or thyme and the reserved bacon.

8 ears fresh corn, shucked
8 slices bacon, chopped
¼ cup (½ stick/55 g) unsalted butter
4 cloves garlic, finely chopped
2 ribs celery, finely chopped
1 yellow onion, finely chopped
1 tablespoon finely chopped fresh thyme
1 fresh or dried bay leaf
6 cups (1.4 L) milk
3 new potatoes (about 1½ pounds/680 g), peeled and cut into ½-inch (12-mm) cubes
Salt and freshly ground black pepper
¼ cup (7 g) thinly sliced fresh basil or 4 sprigs thyme, for serving

GRANDMA BEETSIE'S CHICKEN SOUP

This is my mother's chicken soup recipe. I'm pretty sure it's been passed down from generation to generation to generation. Whenever I was sick as a kid, I got this soup. When I was sad . . . soup. When I was cranky, crampy, moody, heartbroken . . . soup. This soup really is a cure-all. If you like, you can substitute a 16-ounce (455-g) bag of egg noodles for the matzo balls, cooking them and adding them to the soup before serving.

 Serves 4 to 6

1 (4- to 5-pound/1.8- to 2.3-kg)
    whole chicken
8 carrots, peeled and sliced
2 ribs celery, chopped
1 parsnip, peeled and chopped
1 yellow onion, chopped
¼ cup (7 g) chopped fresh dill,
    plus extra for garnish
3 cloves garlic, crushed
2½ cups (290 g) matzo meal
6 large eggs
6 tablespoons (90 ml) vegetable oil
2 teaspoons salt

- Place the chicken in a large pot with the breast-side down. Add the carrots, celery, parsnip, onion, and dill. Fill the pot with enough cold water to cover the chicken and reach about 3 inches (7.5 cm) from the top of the pot. Bring it to a simmer over medium heat and cook, partially covered, for 2 hours. Do not let the soup boil.

- Skim any fat from the top of the soup and add the garlic. Partially cover and simmer for another 2 hours. Remove the chicken to let it cool a bit.

- In a medium bowl, mix together the matzo meal, eggs, oil, salt, and ¼ cup (60 ml) of the broth from the chicken soup. Refrigerate the mixture for about 20 minutes.

- Bring a separate pot of water to a rolling boil. Roll the matzo mixture into about 16 balls. Wet your hands to keep the dough from sticking to them. Drop the balls into boiling water, cover, and cook for about 35 minutes.

- While the matzo balls are cooking, strain the broth from the chicken soup; discard the vegetables. Return the broth to the pot over low heat. Remove the bones and skin from the chicken and cut the meat into bite-size pieces; return it to the broth. Remove the matzo balls from the water, drain them briefly on paper towels, and serve them in the hot chicken soup. Garnish with fresh dill.

FANCY BEEF STEW

This hearty recipe is a guaranteed hit. Everyone, I mean *everyone,* I have made this for has absolutely loved it. Serve it with some great crusty French bread and oven-roasted potatoes. And after your friends and family have eaten this and loved it, you can tell them proudly that you just served them an authentic French *boeuf bourguignon.*

Serves 4

3 pounds (1.4 kg) beef chuck, cut into large pieces

1 large yellow onion, finely chopped

2 carrots, peeled and chopped

2 cloves garlic

1 bouquet garni (see Note)

1 (750-ml) bottle red wine, such as Pinot Noir

6 ounces (170 g) lean salt pork, cut into small pieces

Salt and freshly ground black pepper

⅓ cup (40 g) all-purpose flour

1 pound (455 g) small button mushrooms, trimmed

- Put the beef, onion, carrots, garlic, and bouquet garni in a large bowl. Add the wine. Using your hands, mix all the ingredients together, then cover the bowl with plastic wrap and refrigerate for 24 hours.

- Remove the beef from the marinade, reserving the liquid, and dry the meat well on paper towels. Fry the salt pork in a large pot over medium heat until crisp, about 7 minutes. Season the beef with salt and pepper. Add it to the pot and brown it on all sides, about 7 minutes. Sprinkle with the flour and cook, stirring constantly, for 3 minutes. Add the reserved marinade and 2 cups (480 ml) water and bring them to a boil over high heat, scraping up any brown bits. Reduce the heat to low, cover, and cook until the meat is tender, about 3 hours.

- Add the mushrooms and cook for 30 minutes longer, until the mushrooms are tender. Remove the bouquet garni before serving.

NOTE:

This small flavoring bouquet consists of 1 sprig fresh thyme; 1 bay leaf; 4 sprigs fresh parsley; perhaps a sprig of fresh tarragon or celery leaves; and 4 or 5 peppercorns. Wrap it all up in a bundle of cheesecloth tied closed with kitchen string. Leave the string rather long, and you can tie it to the handle of the pot so it's easy to remove before serving.

EASY-PEASY SPLIT PEA SOUP WITH HAM

When I was on location filming the *Little House* pilot, we went to a restaurant and my mother ordered me split pea soup with ham. It sounded so yummy, and then the bowl came and I was so upset because it looked like blended boogers. I even said so. She talked me into just tasting it, and I discovered that it was the yummiest thing I'd ever eaten.

Serves 4 to 6

- Bring the oil, peas, and 7 cups (1.7 L) water to a boil in a large soup pot. Reduce the heat; cover and simmer for 2 hours, stirring occasionally.

- Add the ham, carrots, celery, onion, potato, salt (if using), garlic powder, and pepper; cover and simmer for 30 minutes, or until the vegetables are tender. Stir in the parsley and serve hot.

1 teaspoon canola oil

1 pound (455 g) dried green split peas (2 cups ml)

2 cups (450 g) cubed cooked ham

2 cups (260 g) chopped carrots

1 cup (100 g) chopped celery

1 cup (120 g) chopped yellow onion

1 cup (150 g) diced peeled potatoes (I prefer russet)

1 teaspoon salt (optional)

½ teaspoon garlic powder

½ teaspoon freshly ground black pepper

¼ cup (7 g) minced fresh parsley

CASSEROLES

MY TOP TEN FAVORITE LITTLE HOUSE EPISODES

One of the questions I get asked most often is, "What is your favorite episode of *Little House on the Prairie*?" It's very hard for me to narrow my answer down to just one episode. We filmed hundreds of hours of the show. So instead of just one, I've narrowed it down to my top ten favorites.

I've put these episodes in no particular order at all. I'll tell you that I watched each of the ten episodes while writing this book to remind me why these are my favorites. Well, I watched all but one. There is one included here that I often refer to as the "Unwatchable One." It's unwatchable because it makes me so, so sad.

1. The Pilot
    I think the pilot episode of *Little House on the Prairie* may well be one of the best made-for-TV movies of all time. It's gripping and fun at the same

time. Its simplicity is very touching. Michael Landon did an extraordinary job as writer, director, executive producer, and star. It's also the only time we shot one complete book from the Laura Ingalls Wilder series. For me, it was (and is) like watching that book come to life right in front of my eyes. I never grow tired of it. I've watched it with all of my children and will gladly share my copy with any of my friends.

Technically, everything about it is spot-on. The costumes, props, set design, hair, and makeup all come together and transport the audience to Kansas in the 1870s. The chemistry among all of the actors is palpable. I guess the best word to describe it is *real*. It's all very real. I defy anyone to watch the pilot movie and not cry at some point.

2. "Country Girls" (season one, episode two)
Whoa, Nellie, and I mean whoa! This episode was a blast. For one thing, there were so many kids around to play with. For another thing, this episode marked the beginning of the epic rivalry between Laura and Nellie. She pushed me. I pushed her. "You wanna fight? I'll fight! You wanna play? We're playing Uncle John!" My youngest son, Michael, watched this episode with me recently. During one of Alison Arngrim's first close-ups in the schoolroom, he said, "Whoa! She looks like she wants to kill you! Slowly!" In real life, this episode marked the beginning of one of the most significant and longest lasting friendships of my life—with Alison Arngrim, my sister from another mother. We are still close to this very day. Also, when you view this episode, watch closely the scene where Ma shows us the fabric for her blue dress. I reached out to touch it, and Melissa Sue Anderson slapped my hand so hard that it made me laugh and then cry. Rewind and watch it again. It's pretty funny.

3. "The Raccoon" (season one, episode ten)
This episode kills me. I cry every time I watch it. I start when Mary confesses to Pa, and I don't stop until after the credits roll. The coolest part, though, is that I got to work with several real live raccoons—babies and adults. I spent crazy amounts of time with the raccoons so we would feel comfortable together. It worked. The scene where Jasper licks my face was pure bliss. That's not acting. That is unadulterated joy on my face! And I got to eat a gumdrop.

4. "The Lord Is My Shepherd" (season one, episodes thirteen and fourteen)
This is one of the stronger, if not the strongest, episodes we ever did. Michael Landon's writing was perfect. Although it's full of important themes about faith and forgiveness, the show is written from a child's

perspective. The fact that Laura literally takes Reverend Alden's advice—"The closer you are to God, the more likely he is to listen"—shows how forceful a simple message can be.

For me personally, this episode was an absolute joy. Working with Ernest Borgnine, Mike, and Victor on location in Sonora, California, was like a dream come true.

The climactic scene where Pa and Laura are reunited on Jonathan's mountain is the quintessential example of my relationship with Mike. The tears were mutual and real. The love between us is clear and obvious. This is the one I just can't bring myself to watch.

5. "At the End of the Rainbow" (season two, episode thirty-four)
All good adventures start with fishing! And what an adventure shooting this episode was. I just adored the dream sequences and dressing up like a prairie princess! Even better were the fun scenes with my costar Shane Sinutko—what a terrific actor. Then there is the scene at the end with Pa and Laura. That scene was one of our best father-daughter moments. Here's a great quote: "Half-Pint, you give us everything we want every single day of our lives. You give us love, respect, and joy; there isn't enough gold in the whole world to buy those things."

Here's a fun little bit of trivia courtesy of our composer, David Rose: When you watch this episode, listen for a bit of a tribute to "Somewhere Over the Rainbow" in the music near the end.

6. "Bunny" (season three, episode forty-eight)
Well, if you thought Nellie was just sort of bad, maybe just a bit spoiled, but really good on the inside, this is the episode that will open your eyes. Nellie is almost borderline in this episode—making her parents believe for weeks that she can't walk. And what she does to poor Laura! Played by any other actor, Nellie could have seemed possessed. Played by Alison Arngrim, she's the girl you love to hate. The wheelchair scene near the end is classic Laura-and-Nellie, second only to the mud fight over Almanzo a season later. The real gem of this episode is Richard Bull's performance as Mr. Oleson—subtle and gentle. The final scene between Richard and me is sweet and very touching. Secret: Alison really broke her arm skateboarding. They put a prairie splint over her cast.

7. "Days of Sunshine, Days of Shadow" (season eight, episodes 176 and 177)
Boy, oh boy, did we keep ol' Doc Baker busy in this episode: diphtheria, a stroke, a baby, a tornado, a nervous breakdown. I actually think they should rename these episodes "Get Doc Baker."

Watching it now with middle-aged eyes, I am so moved by Dean Butler and Lucy Lee Flippin; their work in this episode is so solid. I did my level best too, imagining what it might be like to be married and have a baby. From where I sit now, having lived through those things, I think I might have made different choices as an actor. This may be the first time I had to really reach to play Laura. All that said, there is one line that makes me catch my breath and cry. It's said by Pa to Laura: "Thank you for being my daughter."

8. "The Last Farewell" (television movie)
Filming this remains one of the most powerful yet cathartic experiences of my life! It seems that every day there was a final experience—the last scene in the Mercantile, the last day on the lot, the last time I laced up my boots. As difficult and sad as it was, it was also the perfect way for all of us to say good-bye.

The emotions etched on all of our faces, the sorrow and grief, were absolutely real. This film was our way of celebrating the life of our show and mourning its passing.

9. "Sweet Sixteen" (season six, episode 135)
This episode was shot several months before I turned sixteen myself. This is the episode where the romance between Laura and Almanzo really begins. In fact, they have their first kiss. I remember shooting that kiss and it was a really big deal. It was kind of scary, but it ended up being very sweet and tender. Bless Dean Butler's heart. He was a grown man having to kiss a child. I can only imagine the pressure he felt. If only I'd been able to tell him that I had already kissed a boy in real life—Tim Maier. He played Chad Brewster in that episode. Nobody knew. But they do now!

10. "The Halloween Dream" (season six, episode 120)
This episode was so much fun to shoot! We got to be very silly. There isn't a serious moment in the whole episode. We shot it in Tucson, and here's what's great about that: We shot in old Tucson, which had rides, a candy store, and a shooting gallery. It was crazy hot, but I stayed cool by drinking a lot of root beer floats.

The kid playing the son of Running Bull is Clint "Burkey" Lilley. His dad is Jack Lilley. Burkey is a stunt coordinator now. We've worked together a few times in the past several years.

I watched this episode with my sons recently, and they called me "Knothead" for a whole day!

WORLD PREMIERE

SATURDAY NIGHT · MARCH 30 · NBC TV · SATURDAY NIGHT · MARCH 30

"LITTLE HOUSE ON THE PRAIRIE"

A TWO HOUR FILM VERSION OF THE CLASSIC BY

LAURA INGALLS WILDER

Starring

MICHAEL LANDON

AS CHARLES INGALLS

Directed by **MICHAEL LANDON** · *Executive Producer* **ED FRIENDLY**

LT+AW

Laura's in love.

8:00PM Little House on the Prairie

Her Pa still calls her "Half-pint." But Laura's in love with an older man...and discovers that becoming a woman means more than shedding her pigtails.
Michael Landon
Karen Grassle
Melissa Gilbert
Melissa Sue Anderson

NBC
PROUD AS A PEACOCK

10-YEAR-OLD MELISSA GILBERT TELLS WHY SHE PREFERS GIRLS TO BOYS

Ten-year-old Melissa Gilbert, who plays Laura Ingalls in "Little House on the Prairie," likes girls better than boys.

This revelation came on the top of a mountain above Sonora, Calif., where Melissa was being filmed in a special two-hour episode called "The Lord Is My Shepherd." It will be colorcast on the NBC Television Network Wednesday, Dec. 18 (8-10 p.m. PT).

This fact-based story has to do with the only boy ever born to the Charles Ingalls family. Let Melissa tell it:

"Well, you see, Laura doesn't want the baby to be a boy. She wants it to be a girl. And when it becomes a boy and gets sick, she doesn't pray for it to make it better. It dies and she thinks it's her fault. She runs away, climbs this mountain and says she's going to find God. She finds Jonathan (he's really Ernie Borgnine) who is a very godly man and who says he'll help her talk to God."

Asked if she figured out why Laura did not want a baby brother, Melissa said, "because Pa would pay more attention to him than her."

Melissa's mother, like Laura's also is expecting a baby. Melissa's preference?

"I want it to be a girl. I already have a brother (Jonathan Gilbert, 7, who's also in the series, as Willie Oleson), and besides I like girls more. That's because I'm a girl and I play girls' games. Boys don't play girls' games. I like to play girls' games."

That expected baby had better be a girl. Otherwise Melissa Gilbert might go right back up that mountain. And this time Ernie Borgnine might not be there.

November 26, 1974

Melissa Gilbert and her little sister

Melissa Gilbert

Little House on the Prairie
"The Lord Is My Shepherd"

REAL-DEAL LASAGNA

This may not be American prairie food, but I'll bet it was served often on the frontier in Italy. Remember—they had settlers too! Just picture it: the Leone family sitting around the fire in their Little House in Umbria while Papa plays his violin and Signore Edwards sings that famous Italian song, "Old Danielli Tuckeroni." All of the Leone children laughing and eating mounds of Mama Leone's famous lasagna . . .

There are three steps to making this authentic lasagna recipe. The first is making the basic meat sauce. This is the base of the lasagna and must be made first because it takes time to simmer and develop full flavor. Then you'll make the béchamel sauce, and then you'll assemble and bake the casserole. If you want to be *really* traditional, you could make your own pasta dough, which is not difficult but is very time-consuming. I much prefer to use the no-boil lasagna noodles, which taste great and make the recipe much easier.

 *Serves 6 to 8*

For the Meat Sauce:

¼ to ⅓ cup (60 to 75 ml) olive oil (enough to coat the bottom of your pot)

1 large carrot, peeled and finely chopped

1 rib celery, finely chopped

¼ cup (30 g) chopped onion

2 cloves garlic, minced

1½ pounds (680 g) mix of lean ground beef and ground turkey

Salt and freshly ground black pepper

⅓ cup (75 ml) white wine

2 (28-ounce/800-g) cans crushed tomatoes

1 tablespoon granulated sugar

Make the meat sauce:

- In a large pot over medium heat, add the oil. Then add the carrot, celery, onion, and garlic. Sauté until the onion is translucent and the vegetables have softened, 5 to 8 minutes. Add the meat and sprinkle it with salt and pepper. Cook the meat until brown, 8 to 10 minutes. Add the wine and cook until it has been absorbed into the meat. Add the tomatoes and sugar and mix thoroughly. Reduce the heat to low and simmer for about 2 hours.

Meanwhile, make the béchamel sauce:

- In a saucepan over low heat, melt the butter. Add the flour while stirring constantly. Slowly pour in the milk and continue to stir. (Do not stop stirring the sauce or it will become lumpy.) Add salt and pepper to taste and the nutmeg (if using). Set aside.

For the Béchamel Sauce:

½ cup (1 stick/115 g) unsalted butter
½ cup (60 g) all-purpose flour
3 cups (720 ml) warm whole milk
Salt and freshly ground black pepper
Pinch of ground nutmeg (optional)

Assemble the lasagna:

- Preheat the oven to 400°F (205°C).

- In a deep 9-by-13-inch (23-by-33-cm) baking dish, assemble the lasagna in alternating layers. Begin with a layer of meat sauce, then a layer of pasta, followed by more meat sauce, some mozzarella, some Parmesan, and some béchamel. Continue layering in this order until the dish is full but not overflowing, ending with the béchamel.

- Bake for 30 to 45 minutes, or until the pasta is tender. Let it rest and firm up for about 10 minutes before serving.

For the Assembly:

3 (9-ounce/255-g) boxes no-boil lasagna noodles
6 cups shredded mozzarella cheese (about 1½ pounds/ 690g; more or less depending on preference)
1 cup grated Parmesan cheese (about 3½ pounds/100g; more or less depending on preference)

PASTA WITH MUSHROOM CREAM SAUCE

Let's stay on the Italian prairie for the moment. Mama Leone has been working all day helping Papa Leone pick the grapes for the wine. She is tired and all of the little Leones are hungry. Good thing she dried those porcinis last season! Like Mama Leone, I keep the ingredients for this dish around all the time. It's my go-to dish when I'm working and don't have a lot of time to cook. My family loves this one.

 *Serves 4 to 6*

1 ounce (30 g) dried porcini mushrooms

3 tablespoons olive oil

1 pound (455 g) fresh cremini mushrooms, chopped

8 ounces (225 g) fresh portobello mushrooms, stemmed, dark gills scraped off, chopped

2 cloves garlic, minced

1 dried bay leaf

⅓ cup (75 ml) dry red wine

Salt and freshly ground black pepper

1 pound (455 g) bow tie, fusilli, or penne pasta

1 cup (240 ml) beef broth

¼ cup (60 ml) heavy whipping cream

1 cup freshly grated Parmesan cheese (about 3½ ounces/100g), plus more for serving

2 tablespoons unsalted butter

- Put the porcini mushrooms in a small bowl and pour hot water over them. Let them stand until the mushrooms soften, about 25 minutes. Using a slotted spoon, transfer the mushrooms to a work surface and coarsely chop. Discard the soaking liquid.

- Heat the oil in a large heavy pot over medium-high heat. Add the chopped porcini, the cremini and portobello mushrooms, garlic, and bay leaf. Sauté until the mushrooms are brown and tender, stirring often, about 10 minutes. Add the wine and simmer until almost all the liquid evaporates, scraping up any browned bits, about 1 minute. Season the mushroom mixture to taste with salt and pepper. Remove from the heat.

- Cook the pasta in a large pot of boiling salted water until just tender but still firm to the bite, stirring occasionally. Drain well.

- Stir the broth and cream into the mushroom mixture, put it back on the stove over medium heat, and simmer for 3 minutes. Add the Parmesan, butter, and drained pasta; toss to coat. Cook, stirring frequently, about 2 minutes. Discard the bay leaf and season to taste with salt and pepper. Serve hot, with more Parmesan.

FAVORITE MACARONI AND CHEESE

I adore macaroni and cheese. Whenever I see it on a menu at a restaurant, I have to order it. I've had (and consequently made) fried mac and cheese balls, lobster mac and cheese, truffle mac and cheese, *quattro formaggi* mac and cheese, and Kraft mac and cheese. Now, don't get me wrong—all of the fancy macaroni and cheese dishes have been delectable and enjoyable, but at home, I like a simple, delicious mac and cheese. So here's my recipe. This dish is best when served during a game or movie night with family and friends.

Serves 8 to 10

- Preheat the oven to 350°F (175°C). Grease a 9-by-13-inch (23-by-33-cm) baking dish. Bring a 4-quart (3.8-L) saucepan of salted water to a boil. Add the pasta and cook it halfway through, about 3 minutes. Drain the pasta and transfer it to the baking dish. Stir in the cubed Velveeta.

- Combine the flour, salt, mustard, black pepper, nutmeg, and cayenne in a large mixing bowl. Add the sour cream and eggs and whisk until smooth. Whisk in the half-and-half, cream, onion, Worcestershire sauce, and a sprinkle of black pepper. Pour the egg mixture over the pasta mixture in the prepared baking dish and stir to combine. Sprinkle the Cheddar cheese evenly over the surface. Bake until the pasta mixture is set around the edges but still a bit loose in the center, about 30 minutes. Let it cool for 10 minutes before serving.

8 ounces (225 g) elbow macaroni

1½ cups Velveeta cheese (about 7 ounces/190g), cut into ½-inch cubes

2 tablespoons plus 1 teaspoon all-purpose flour

1½ teaspoons kosher salt

1½ teaspoons dry mustard

¼ teaspoon freshly ground black pepper

¼ teaspoon ground nutmeg

⅛ teaspoon cayenne pepper

⅔ cup (165 ml) sour cream

2 large eggs, lightly beaten

1½ cups (360 ml) half-and-half

1½ cups (360 ml) heavy cream

⅓ cup (55 g) grated onion

1 teaspoon Worcestershire sauce

2 cups grated sharp Cheddar cheese (about 8 ounces/230g)

MY TUNA-NOODLE CASSEROLE

I cook a lot—sometimes very fancy, intricate meals. I can spend upward of two to three days preparing and cooking a meal. And by and large, my family loves my food. We've had Italian nights, Asian nights, homemade sushi nights, taco bar nights, breakfast-for-dinner nights—you name it, we've done it. Sometimes the kids are reluctant to show up. Unless I tell them it's Tuna-Noodle Casserole night. Then they come running and usually bring friends, so I'm forever doubling, even tripling, this dish. It's a great dish to drop off with a friend who isn't feeling well, or to give to a friend or relative with a new baby at home. It's especially comforting for someone going through grief. Quite simply, this is the *Best. Dish. Ever.* There's not a kid of any age in the world who won't love it, I promise. If you want to get a little fancy, use imported Italian tuna. This casserole is really yummy served cold the next day—or even later the same night! Save the crusty parts for me, please. . . .

 *continued*

1 yellow onion, finely chopped

4½ tablespoons (65 g) unsalted butter

¼ teaspoon plus a pinch of salt, plus more if needed

10 ounces (280 g) button mushrooms, trimmed and sliced ¼ inch (6 mm) thick

2 teaspoons soy sauce

¼ cup (60 ml) sherry

¼ cup (30 g) all-purpose flour

2 cups (480 ml) low-sodium chicken broth

1 cup (240 ml) whole milk

2 teaspoons freshly squeezed lemon juice

1 (6-oz/170-g) can tuna in olive oil, drained

Freshly ground black pepper

6 ounces (170 g) curly egg noodles (preferably Pennsylvania Dutch style)

1½ cups (80 g) coarse fresh bread crumbs (from 3 slices firm white sandwich bread)

1 cup coarsely grated Cheddar cheese (about 4 ounces/115g)

1 tablespoon vegetable oil

- Preheat the oven to 375°F (190°C) and position a rack in the middle. Butter a shallow 2-quart (2-L) baking dish.

- In a large heavy skillet over moderate heat, cook the onion in 1½ tablespoons of the butter with a pinch of salt, stirring occasionally, until softened, about 5 minutes. Increase the heat to medium-high and add the mushrooms. Sauté, stirring occasionally, for about 2 minutes. Add the soy sauce and continue to sauté, stirring, until the liquid has evaporated. Add the sherry and boil, stirring occasionally, until evaporated. Remove from the heat.

- Melt the remaining 3 tablespoons of butter in a 2- to 3-quart (2- to 2.8-L) heavy saucepan over medium heat and whisk in the flour, then cook, whisking constantly, for 3 minutes to make a roux. Add the broth in a stream, whisking constantly, and bring to a boil. Whisk in the milk and simmer the sauce, whisking occasionally, for 5 minutes. Stir in the mushroom mixture, lemon juice, and ¼ teaspoon salt. Flake the tuna into the sauce and stir gently. Season with salt and pepper to taste.

- Cook the noodles in a large pot of boiling salted water until al dente. Drain and return them to the pot. Add the sauce and stir gently to combine. Transfer the mixture to the baking dish, spreading it evenly.

- Toss together the bread crumbs and cheese in a medium bowl. Drizzle them with the oil, toss again, then sprinkle them evenly over the casserole. Bake until the topping is crisp and the sauce is bubbling, 20 to 30 minutes. Serve hot.

VEGETABLE SOUFFLÉ

The word *soufflé* can strike fear in the heart of many a home cook. It certainly made me shake in my boots the first time I made one, but if you follow the directions carefully and *don't open the oven door until it's done*, you'll be just fine. Your family and friends will be thoroughly impressed by this dish, and it's a really good way to get some veggies into those finicky kids. You can use all one vegetable, or use a combination.

Serves 4

- Preheat the oven to 350°F (175°C).

- In a medium saucepan over medium heat, melt the butter and cook the onion and garlic in the butter until tender, 2 to 3 minutes. Stir in the flour, marjoram, salt, and pepper. Add the milk all at once. Cook and stir for about 10 minutes, or until thickened and bubbly. Remove from the heat. Add the cheese and stir until melted. Stir in the cooked vegetables.

- In a large bowl, beat the egg yolks with a fork until combined. Gradually add the vegetable mixture, stirring constantly.

- In a separate large bowl, beat the egg whites until stiff peaks form (tips stand straight up). Gently fold about 1 cup (240 ml) of the beaten egg whites into the vegetable mixture to lighten it. Gradually pour the vegetable mixture over the remaining beaten egg whites, folding to combine. Pour the batter into an ungreased 1½-quart (1.4-L) soufflé dish or a 6-by-10-by-2-inch (15-by-25-by-5-cm) baking dish.

- Bake for about 40 minutes for the soufflé dish or 25 to 30 minutes for the baking dish, or until a knife inserted near the center comes out clean. Serve immediately.

3 tablespoons unsalted butter

¼ cup (30 g) chopped onion

1 clove garlic, minced

¼ cup (30 g) all-purpose flour

¾ teaspoon chopped fresh marjoram, basil, dill, or tarragon

¼ teaspoon salt

¼ teaspoon freshly ground black pepper

1 cup (240 ml) warm whole milk

1 cup shredded Cheddar or Swiss cheese (about 4 ounces/115g)

1 cup (about 90 g) finely chopped cooked broccoli, cauliflower, asparagus, carrot, and/or spinach

3 large eggs, separated

INDIVIDUAL CHICKEN POTPIES

One of the go-to meals on *Little House* was chicken potpie. It's also a family favorite around here because I really like the convenience of a one-dish meal. This recipe has everything in it, so you can rest assured that everyone in your family is getting all of the vitamins and minerals they need. I deviate from the traditional a bit with the puff pastry top, but my family loves the flakiness of it, and I love the fact that it doesn't have quite the calorie count of a regular pastry crust.

Serves 4

- Preheat the oven to 425°F (220°C).

- Place the chicken pieces, onion, celery, and chopped carrots in a large stockpot; season with salt and pepper and add enough water to cover. Wrap the thyme and garlic in a piece of cheesecloth and tie it with kitchen twine to enclose, then tie the twine to the pot handle so you don't have to fish around for it; add it to the pot. Cover the pot and place it over medium heat; bring to a boil. Reduce the heat to a simmer and cook until the chicken is no longer pink, about 25 minutes. Strain the broth, discarding the vegetables and herbs in the cheesecloth (the bouquet garni), and reserve the chicken and broth separately; set aside to let cool.

- Bring a medium pot of salted water to a boil and prepare an ice-water bath. Add the baby carrots to the boiling water and cook until tender, about 5 minutes. Using a slotted spoon, strain them out and immediately transfer them to the ice-water bath until cool. Drain and set aside. Put the peas in the boiling water and cook for about 30 seconds; strain them out and set aside. Add the pearl onions to the boiling water and cook for about 1 minute; drain them and transfer them to the ice-water bath until cool. Drain and set aside.

4 boneless, skinless chicken breast halves
4 boneless, skinless chicken thighs
1 medium yellow onion, coarsely chopped
2 ribs celery, cut into 1-inch (2.5-cm) pieces
3 carrots, coarsely chopped
Salt and freshly ground black pepper
4 sprigs fresh thyme
2 cloves garlic, crushed
1 cup (130 g) baby carrots
1 cup (135 g) frozen green peas
1 cup (115 g) fresh or frozen pearl onions
4 tablespoons plus 1 teaspoon (60 g) unsalted butter
2½ cups (220 g) cremini mushrooms, trimmed and cut into quarters
¼ cup (30 g) all-purpose flour
2 cups (480 ml) heavy cream
1 teaspoon Tabasco sauce
1½ teaspoons Worcestershire sauce
2 sheets frozen puff pastry (from a 17-ounce/485-g package)
1 large egg, beaten

continued

- Heat 1 teaspoon of the butter in a medium skillet over medium heat. Add the mushrooms and cook until browned, 3 to 4 minutes; let cool.

- Cut the chicken into bite-size pieces and place them in a large heat-proof bowl along with the baby carrots, peas, pearl onions, and mushrooms.

- In a medium skillet, heat the remaining 4 tablespoons (55 g) of butter. Add the flour and cook, stirring, for 1 minute. Add ½ cup (120 ml) of the reserved cooking broth and the cream. Cook, stirring constantly, until the liquid comes to a boil. Reduce the heat to a simmer and cook for 2 minutes. Remove from the heat and add the Tabasco and Worcestershire sauces; season with salt and pepper. Add the liquid to the bowl with chicken and vegetables, tossing to combine.

- Divide the mixture evenly among four 13-ounce (390-ml) shallow baking dishes. Cut the puff pastry into four 8-inch (20-cm) circles and place one on top of each of the baking dishes, crimping the edges. Cut a slit in the center of each piece of puff pastry; brush the beaten egg over the puff pastry.

- Transfer the baking dishes to a rimmed baking sheet. Bake for about 25 minutes, until the puff pastry is golden brown and the filling is bubbling. Let stand for 5 minutes before serving.

STEAK, POTATO, AND LEEK PIES

There's something very prairie about a savory dinner pie. About all pies, in fact. I can't make a homemade piecrust to save my life, but I do love pie, and these individual hand pies are divine. So thank you, whoever invented the modern refrigerated piecrust. Serve this with Greeny McGreen Green Salad (page 142) on the side.

 *continued*

3 tablespoons unsalted butter

2 (6-ounce/170-g) beef tenderloin steaks

Salt and freshly ground black pepper

1¾ cups (260 g) red-skin potato cubes (⅓-inch/8-mm)

1½ cups (135 g) chopped leeks (white and pale green parts only)

½ teaspoon dry mustard

1 tablespoon steak sauce

2 large scallions, chopped

4 (9-inch/23-cm) refrigerated piecrusts, warmed to room temperature (Not in pie tins; you'll find the ones I'm talking about in the dairy section of your local supermarket.)

1 large egg, beaten

- Melt 1 tablespoon of the butter in a medium skillet over medium-high heat. Sprinkle the steaks with salt and pepper. Add the steaks to the skillet and cook until medium-rare, about 4 minutes per side. Transfer the steaks to a cutting board and cut them into ½-inch (12-mm) cubes.

- Melt the remaining 2 tablespoons butter in the skillet. Add the potatoes, leeks, and mustard. Cook and stir for 1 minute. Reduce the heat to medium, cover, and cook until the potatoes are tender, stirring occasionally, about 8 minutes.

- Return the beef and any accumulated juices to the skillet. Add the steak sauce and sauté for 2 minutes. Remove the skillet from the heat and stir in the scallions. Season the filling to taste with salt and pepper. Let it cool completely.

- Preheat the oven to 400°F (205°C). Unfold the piecrusts on a work surface. Cut each crust into two pieces along the center fold. Brush the dough with the beaten egg. Place ½ cup (120 ml) of the filling on half of each piece. Fold the untopped side of the dough over the filling and crimp the crust closed with a fork to seal the edges. Brush the tops of the pies with more egg and arrange them on two baking sheets.

- Bake the pies for 15 minutes, then switch the baking sheets and continue baking until the crusts are golden and the filling is heated through, about 10 minutes longer. Let the pies cool on wire racks for a few minutes before serving.

SHEPHERD'S PIE

This recipe is one of my all-time favorite family meals. It is a complete meal unto itself and a big hit with kids and adults alike. If you want, you can substitute ground lamb, beef, turkey, chicken, or soy meat for the lamb cubes (or any combination of them), but please try it first with the cubed lamb. You won't be sorry!

Serves 4 to 6

- Melt about 2 tablespoons of the butter in a large Dutch oven. Sauté the lamb in batches until brown on all sides, adding a bit more butter if needed as you go. Transfer the cooked lamb to a platter as it browns.

- Add the carrots and leeks to the Dutch oven, and cook until soft. Return the lamb and any accumulated juices to the pot. Sprinkle with the flour and stir for 1 minute. Whisk in the broth, Worcestershire sauce, thyme, nutmeg, and salt and pepper. Cook until thickened, about 45 minutes. Stir in the peas and remove from the heat.

- Meanwhile, boil the potatoes in a pot of salted water until tender. Drain and put them in a mixing bowl. Add the remaining butter (reserving 1 tablespoon), the half-and-half (as needed), and salt and pepper and mash until smooth.

- Preheat the oven to 375°F (190°C). Top the lamb mixture in the Dutch oven with the mashed potatoes. Cut the remaining 1 tablespoon butter into small bits and scatter over the potatoes. Bake uncovered for about 30 minutes, or until golden and bubbling. Serve hot.

1 cup (2 sticks/225 g) unsalted butter
2 pounds (910 g) lamb shoulder, cut into cubes
2 carrots, chopped
2 leeks (white parts only), chopped
2 tablespoons all-purpose flour
1½ cups (360 ml) beef broth
1 tablespoon Worcestershire sauce
1 tablespoon chopped fresh thyme or rosemary leaves
Pinch of ground nutmeg
Salt and freshly ground black pepper
1 (16-ounce/455-g) bag frozen peas, thawed
3 large russet potatoes (about 1½ pounds/680 g), cut into chunks
½ to 1 cup (120 to 240 ml) half-and-half

SCALLOPED POTATO AND HAM CASSEROLE

Prairie-style satisfaction: butter, potatoes, ham . . . in a casserole. Do not ask why; merely ask, why not?

Serves 6 to 8

6 to 8 russet potatoes
¼ cup (½ stick/55 g) unsalted
    butter
3 tablespoons all-purpose flour
1 teaspoon salt
½ teaspoon freshly ground black
    pepper
2½ cups (600 ml) warm milk
1 small yellow onion, chopped
1 to 1½ pounds (455 to 680 g)
    ham, cubed

- Preheat the oven to 350°F (175°C). Butter a 2-quart (2-L) casserole dish.

- Cut the potatoes into thin slices to measure about 4 cups (960 ml; I use a mandoline for this).

- Melt 3 tablespoons of the butter in a medium sauce-pan over low heat. Stir in the flour, salt, and pepper and cook, stirring constantly, until the mixture is smooth and bubbly, about 5 minutes. Remove it from the heat and stir in the milk. Return the pan to the stove and bring it to a boil, stirring constantly; boil and stir for about 1 minute.

- Arrange the potatoes in the casserole dish in lay-ers, topping each layer of potatoes with some of the onion, white sauce, and ham. End with a layer of potatoes and dot the top layer with the remaining 1 tablespoon butter.

- Cover and bake for 30 minutes. Uncover and bake for 60 to 70 minutes longer, until the potatoes are tender. Let stand for about 10 minutes before serving.

MAIN COURSES

LITTLE HOUSE:
THE LATER YEARS

The later years of *Little House* were an odd time for me and for the rest of the cast. We were all young in real life, yet we were getting hitched and having babies on screen. Laura married Almanzo, Mary married Adam, and even Nellie and Willie managed to tie the knot (not to each other! Ew!) in some pretty classic episodes. But I have to be perfectly honest: Once I turned seventeen in real life and had my first boyfriend, prairie life began to lose its charm. I wanted to be cool, cut my hair so I looked like everybody else, and hang out with my friends. You know, do teenager stuff. Instead, I was stuck with my hair parted in the middle and all one length, and I spent the majority of my time in pantaloons and lace-up granny boots.

Looking back now, and having performed in the *Little House on the Prairie* musical as an adult, I totally get the charm of the pantaloons, boots, and petticoats. The "prairie naked" look can be very appealing on a woman of a certain age! (Yes, I mean me!) That said, when I was seventeen, in 1981, prairie wear was just not cool—unless it was designed by Ralph Lauren, and even then, there was no way I'd wear that stuff in public. I was trying to have a private life, which was already impossible. So I rebelled a bit: tight jeans, cut-up T-shirts. And I even started sneaking a little Sun-In in my hair. If you're old enough to remember that stuff, welcome to my generation. My hair was naturally aubern-y red, and the Sun-In turned it a lovely shade of orange. Looking back, this rebellion seems really mild. The part that was really hard was that I really didn't want to go to work every single day. I wanted playtime, freedom with my boyfriend (what's-his-name), and my car.

Still, I showed up, suited up, and managed to have some amazing times. It never failed to amaze me that no matter how much I didn't want to go, once I got to work I was completely at home. That set was my happy place. It's where I felt safe and loved, even in the heated emotional and brutal heart of adolescence.

It seemed as if *Little House* would never end—that it would go on like that forever. When season nine came, Mike left the show as an actor. I was bumped up to number one on our call sheet, and the title was changed to *Little House: A New Beginning*. For all intents and purposes, the show felt as if it were mine. I felt responsible for its success or failure, and at the same time it seemed like a perfectly natural progression. Not much had really changed. New cast mates came in, but our set life remained the same.

But I'll never, ever forget one day that Victor French called me to ask if I would do a talk show with him to protest the cancellation. I said, "Sure, what cancellation?" I hadn't gotten the official word from NBC, so I had no idea. It turned out that no one did. Not even Mike and Kent. We were all basically handed our pink slips, told to pack up our dressing rooms, and say good-bye. Fortunately, someone had the good sense to slow things down and film the three "farewell" movies. Each of those movies was emotional and cathartic in its own way. The final one, called "Little House: The Last Farewell," was, for me, more than a movie. That film marks the beginning of another major turning point in my life: the end of my childhood. It was time for me to leave the nest and try my wings.

These photos are all from the very last day of filming. If you look close enough, you can see the tears ... if you look even closer you can see the joy and the gratitude.

GENERAL GILBERT'S CALIFORNIA FRIED CHICKEN WITH PAN GRAVY

⊰⊰•◦•⊱⊱

We ate a lot of fried chicken on *Little House*. Seems like it was a part of nearly every picnic or dinner scene we did. The creative team wanted everything on our show to be authentic. It was up to the men in the prop department to keep everything looking right, and so they served us buckets full of Kentucky Fried Chicken! *Huh?* Cross my heart, it's true: The fried chicken we ate on *Little House on the Prairie* was from KFC.

My fried chicken, however, is the real deal. Whenever I ask friends or family what they want me to make for dinner, nine times out of ten it's my fried chicken. No offense to Colonel Sanders, but General Gilbert's recipe is better. And it's not a secret. Eleven herbs and spices, my lily-white Irish butt!

 *continued*

Serves 4 to 6, with enough for cold leftovers!

2 cups plus 2 tablespoons (270 g)
    all-purpose flour
5 tablespoons (45 g) Old Bay
    Seasoning
2 tablespoons salt
1 tablespoon freshly ground black
    pepper
2 (4- to 5-pound/1.8- to 2.3-g)
    fryer chickens, cut into pieces,
    rinsed, and patted dry
Vegetable oil, for frying
2 cups (480 ml) warm milk

- Mix 2 cups (250 g) of the flour, the Old Bay, salt, and pepper in a large zip-top bag. Drop in the chicken pieces (you will probably have to do this in batches) and shake to coat.

- Pour the oil into a deep 12-inch (30.5-cm) cast-iron skillet to a depth of 1 inch (2.5 cm). Heat it over high heat until a drop of water bubbles. Shake any excess seasoning mix off the chicken and put it skin-side down in the pan, cooking in batches, if necessary, to avoid overcrowding. Cook on one side for 15 minutes, then turn the chicken pieces over and fry uncovered for another 15 minutes, or until golden brown. Drain the chicken on paper towels. Keep it warm in a low oven while you finish frying all of the chicken.

- Pour off the oil from the skillet, leaving approximately 3 tablespoons in the skillet, and turn the heat to medium. Add the remaining 2 tablespoons flour to the skillet while whisking, mixing in the crunchy bits and cooking for 5 minutes. Pour in the milk and bring it to a low boil, whisking constantly and cooking for another 2 minutes. Season with salt and pepper to taste and serve with the fried chicken.

CRISPY CHICKEN WITH SHERRY VINEGAR SAUCE

This dish is really simple, but the flavors are so vivid—especially if you can use a good-quality Spanish sherry vinegar. If you wish, halve the recipe for a great main dish for a romantic dinner for two. Not long after I made this meal for my husband, Tim, he proposed. After all of the crying and jumping up and down, I asked him what made him decide to propose. "It was the chicken," he joked. They say the way to a man's heart is through his stomach. This recipe proves that to be true.

Serves 4

- Preheat the oven to 450°F (230°C). Pat the chicken dry and sprinkle it evenly with 1 teaspoon of salt and the pepper.

- Heat the oil in a 12-inch (30.5-cm) heavy skillet over medium-high heat until hot but not smoking, then sear the chicken, skin-side down, until golden brown, 4 to 6 minutes. Transfer the chicken, skin-side up, with tongs to a large shallow baking pan (reserve the skillet) and roast it until the chicken is just cooked through, 20 to 25 minutes. Remove from the oven and let stand for 5 minutes.

- Meanwhile, cook the garlic in the reserved skillet over medium-high heat, stirring, until pale golden, 15 to 30 seconds. Add the paprika, then immediately add the vinegar, stirring and scraping up any brown bits, and boil it for 1 minute. Add the broth and honey and simmer, stirring occasionally, until the liquid is reduced to about ½ cup (120 ml), about 2 minutes. Remove from the heat and whisk in the butter, 1 tablespoon at a time, until incorporated. Season the sauce with salt if desired and serve over the chicken.

4 skin-on, bone-in chicken breast halves (about 2 pounds/910 g total)
1 teaspoon salt, plus more for seasoning
½ teaspoon freshly ground black pepper
2 tablespoons olive oil
4 garlic cloves, finely chopped
¾ teaspoon paprika
⅓ cup (75 ml) sherry vinegar
⅓ cup (75 ml) reduced-sodium chicken broth
2 teaspoons mild honey
2 tablespoons unsalted butter

RICH CHICKEN AND DUMPLINGS

The definitive prairie food, this is rich and rib-sticking. I think that whenever we weren't eating fried chicken in food scenes, we were eating chicken and dumplings! My recipe adds a little zing to the traditional version. Don't be freaked out by the amount of butter listed in the ingredients. I know it's a lot, but you'll be very happy when you taste the end result—incredibly light and buttery dumplings.

 *Serves 8*

1 (4-pound/1.8-kg) whole chicken
4 ounces (115 g) slab bacon, cut into slivers
2 tablespoons canola oil
4 carrots, thickly sliced
4 ribs celery, thickly sliced
2 yellow onions, cut into 1-inch (2.5-cm) chunks
4 cloves garlic, chopped
2 teaspoons dried thyme
1 fresh or dried bay leaf
2⅔ cups (330 g) all-purpose flour
1 cup (240 ml) white wine
1 tablespoon baking powder
½ teaspoon baking soda
1½ teaspoons salt, plus more for seasoning
¼ teaspoon freshly ground black pepper, plus more for seasoning
5½ cups (11 sticks/1.25 kg) unsalted butter, melted and cooled slightly (I know!)
¾ cup (180 ml) buttermilk
2 tablespoons finely chopped fresh parsley

• Remove and halve the chicken legs, separating the thighs from the drumsticks; season with salt and pepper and set aside. Put the remaining chicken into a large pot; cover it with salted water and bring to a boil. Reduce the heat and simmer until the breast is just cooked, 12 to 15 minutes. Remove the chicken from the pot. Cut the breasts and wings from the carcass. Discard any skin and bones from the breast and wing meat; cut it into 1-inch (2.5-cm) chunks and refrigerate.

• Return the carcass to the pot, and simmer it for 1 hour. Strain the broth, reserving 1 quart (960 ml) of the broth.

• Meanwhile, cook the bacon in a large wide pot over medium heat until crisp, 8 to 10 minutes. Transfer the bacon to a plate; leave the fat in the pot. Add and heat the oil, then brown the drumsticks and thighs, 8 to 10 minutes. Transfer them to a plate.

- Add the carrots, celery, onions, garlic, thyme, and bay leaf to the pot; cook until they are light brown, 18 to 20 minutes. Add ⅔ cup (80 g) of the flour and cook for 1 minute. Add the wine and cook for 1 minute. Whisk in the reserved broth and salt and pepper to taste. Nestle in the drumsticks, thighs, and bacon pieces. Reduce the heat to medium-low and simmer, covered, for 15 minutes.

- In a large bowl, whisk together the remaining 2 cups (250 g) of flour, the baking powder, baking soda, 1½ teaspoons of salt, and ¼ teaspoon of pepper. Combine the butter, buttermilk, and parsley in a separate bowl; pour them into the flour mixture and stir to make a thick batter.

- Uncover the pot and add the breast and wing meat. Drop the batter in 8 large spoonfuls over the top. Simmer, covered, until the dumplings are cooked, 20 to 25 minutes. Discard the dried bay leaf (if using) and serve immediately.

ROAST CHICKEN
WITH SAGE AND GARLIC

You can never go wrong with roast chicken—its goodness is timeless. Save as much left-over meat as you can get off the bones and mix it up with a bit of mayo, chopped celery, chopped scallions, and some salt and pepper, and you'll have a delicious chicken salad. Or use the bones and leftover meat to make broth.

Serves 4 to 6

- Preheat the oven to 475°F (240°C). Rinse the chicken under cold water; pat it dry with paper towels.

- Peel the lemon, then quarter it and set aside. Finely chop the lemon peel, sage, and garlic together, and place them in a small bowl. Add the butter and 1 teaspoon salt, and stir to combine.

- Loosen the skin of the chicken from the breasts and thighs. Slip the butter mixture between the skin and flesh, spreading it evenly. Rub the skin with the oil; season the skin and cavity with salt and pepper. Stuff the cavity with the quartered lemon, parsley, and 1 quartered onion. Tie the legs together with kitchen string.

- Put the remaining quartered onion and the carrots into the center of a roasting pan and place the chicken on top of them. Roast for 20 minutes, then reduce the oven temperature to 400°F (205°C) and continue roasting until an instant-read thermometer inserted into the thickest part of the thigh reads 165°F (75°C), about 1 hour more.

- Transfer the chicken to a platter, sprinkle it with sea salt, and let it rest for 10 minutes before carving.

1 (4-pound/1.8-kg) whole chicken
1 lemon
22 fresh sage leaves
3 cloves garlic, peeled
6 tablespoons (¾ stick/85 g) unsalted butter, at room temperature
1 teaspoon salt, plus more for seasoning
2 tablespoons olive oil
Freshly ground black pepper
8 sprigs fresh parsley
2 small yellow onions, quartered
2 carrots, cut into 2-inch (5-cm) pieces
Coarse sea salt

ROAST TURKEY WITH HERB BUTTER

———⟨⟐⟩———

We never did a Thanksgiving episode of *Little House* because it had been declared a national holiday only a few years before the show takes place! But Thanksgiving is my favorite holiday of all, mainly because my favorite meal is served on that day. In fact, I like to make that meal a few times a year—usually when I'm feeling especially grateful. I also like to make a roast turkey meal and take it to friends with newborn babies. It's the perfect meal because it's plentiful and so much can be done with the leftovers.

 Serves 8 to 12

1 (12-pound/5.4 kg) turkey
(preferably organic)
1 cup (225 g) Herb Butter (recipe
opposite)
4 cups (about 800 g) stuffing,
homemade (see page 156)
or store-bought prepared
according to package
instructions
Salt and freshly ground black
pepper
4 stalks celery, sliced
2 carrots, sliced
1 yellow onion, sliced
2 cups (480 ml) chicken broth
2 oranges, sliced

- About 5 hours before serving time, remove the giblets and neck from inside the turkey cavity. Rinse the bird inside and out with cold water; pat dry. Slide a rubber spatula between the skin and breast meat to separate them. Stuff half of the herb butter under the skin of both breasts, spreading it evenly over the entire breast area with your fingertips. Rub the remaining butter over the skin of the rest of the bird.

- Fill the cavity loosely with the stuffing. Truss the bird with kitchen string and season it with salt and pepper.

- Spread the celery, carrots, and onion over the bottom of a large roasting pan. Lay the turkey on top, breast-side up. Add 1 cup (240 ml) of the broth to the pan.

- About 4 hours before serving time, preheat the oven to 375°F (190°C); position a rack in the lower half of the oven. Roast the turkey for 1½ hours, turning the pan every 30 minutes or so to ensure that the turkey is browning evenly, and adding more of the broth if the liquid evaporates below ¼ inch (6 mm) in the pan. (If the turkey browns too rapidly, create a tent with aluminum foil and drape it over the turkey breast for the remainder of the roasting time.)

- Reduce the temperature to 325°F (165°C) and roast for 1½ to 2 hours more. Use a thermometer to test the internal temperature of a thigh—it's cooked through when the stuffing and thigh meat reach 165°F (75°C).

- Let the turkey rest for 30 minutes before carving. When ready to serve, garnish the turkey with the orange slices.

HERB BUTTER

- Place all of the ingredients in a food processor and blend. Transfer the butter to a small bowl. Set it aside (or make it a day ahead and refrigerate).

Makes about 1 cup (225 g)

½ cup (1 stick/115 g) unsalted
    butter, softened
¼ cup (60 ml) extra-virgin olive oil
1 tablespoon freshly squeezed
    lemon juice
1 tablespoon chopped shallot
1 tablespoon chopped garlic
¼ cup (7 g) chopped fresh parsley
1 tablespoon chopped fresh chives
1 tablespoon chopped fresh sage
1 tablespoon chopped fresh thyme
1 teaspoon chopped fresh tarragon

PORKY CHOPS AND APPLEYSAUCE

When I was a girl, my food intake was somewhat restricted. Not overly so, but we ate very health-conscious foods. Fried foods were certainly a rare treat. While on location shooting *Little House*, though, we ate in restaurants quite a bit, and in those situations, all restrictions were off. One of my favorite things to order was pan-fried pork chops with a side of applesauce. I look back on those days with such fondness. Everything was an adventure, even mealtime. This recipe is an homage to that magical time in my life. Serve with a side of Best Stuffing Ever (page 156), as I do here, for a delicious and comforting meal.

Serves 4

For the Marinade:

2 cups (480 ml) milk

2 teaspoons salt

4 (½-inch/12-mm-thick) pork
  chops, with or without the bone
  (about 2 pounds/910 g total)

For the Applesauce:

3 pounds (1.4 kg) mixed apples

3 tablespoons granulated sugar

1 tablespoon apple-cider vinegar

1 dried bay leaf

¼ teaspoon ground allspice

- Marinate the pork chops: Stir together the milk and salt in a shallow 3-quart (2.8-L) dish, then add the pork chops. Marinate them, covered and refrigerated and turning over once, for at least 1 hour.

- Make the applesauce: While the chops marinate, peel, core, and chop the apples, then stir them together with the sugar, vinegar, bay leaf, and allspice in a heavy 3-quart (2.8-L) saucepan. Bring them to a simmer, stirring occasionally, then reduce the heat to medium-low and cook, covered, stirring occasionally, until the apples are falling apart, 15 to 20 minutes. Discard the bay leaf and mash the apples with a fork. Keep the applesauce warm.

continued

For the Pork Chops:

3½ cups (190 g) fresh bread
  crumbs (from 10 slices firm
  white sandwich bread, ground
  in a food processor)
1 tablespoon minced garlic
2 teaspoons chopped fresh
  rosemary
2 teaspoons chopped fresh thyme
1 teaspoon salt
2 to 3 tablespoons vegetable oil
2 to 3 tablespoons unsalted butter

- Fry the pork chops: Preheat the oven to 200°F (90°C).

- Stir together the bread crumbs, garlic, rosemary, thyme, and salt in a shallow bowl. Lift the pork chops from the milk one at a time, letting any excess drip off, and dredge them in the bread crumbs, lightly patting the crumbs on to help them adhere. Transfer the chops to a tray in a single layer.

- Heat 2 tablespoons of the oil and 2 tablespoons of the butter in a 12-inch (30.5-cm) heavy skillet over medium-high heat. Sauté the chops in 2 or 3 batches, without crowding, turning them over once, until golden brown and just cooked through, 5 to 6 minutes per batch. Transfer them to a platter and keep warm in the oven. Add more oil and butter to the skillet as needed.

- Serve the pork chops with the warm applesauce.

APPLEYSAUCE

BEST STUFFING EVER

PORKY CHOPS

MG'S BARBECUED RIBS

I've made this dish many times for friends and family. I love to watch everyone get covered in barbecue sauce. (Keep plenty of paper towels around.) It's great at home or on a camping trip, at the beach, wherever. Serve with Mikey B's Favorite Fried Corn (page 149) and Cucumber-Dill Salad (page 139). These ribs are also amazing served cold the next day. You can make your own barbecue sauce if you have a favorite recipe. I like to mix three or four different bottled barbecue sauces together to create my own signature sauce; it's a lot of fun to blend different flavor combinations each time.

Serves 4 to 6

4 dried bay leaves
¼ cup (75 g) garlic salt
¼ cup (30 g) Old Bay Seasoning
¼ cup (30 g) onion powder
¼ cup (30 g) paprika
¼ cup (75 g) seasoned salt
¼ cup (30 g) ground celery seed
¼ cup (30 g) dry mustard
2 tablespoons ground cumin
2 racks baby back ribs (about 2 pounds/910 g each), membrane on back of ribs removed
3 cups (720 ml) barbecue sauce

- Fill a large pot with cold water, stir in all of the spices, put the ribs in the pot, and weigh them down so they are submerged (I use a small stainless-steel frying pan that fits into the pot). Bring the water to a boil, then lower the heat and simmer for 45 minutes.

- Meanwhile, preheat a gas or charcoal grill to high.

- Remove the ribs from the pot and discard the liquid. Grill the ribs for 20 minutes per side, basting with some of the barbecue sauce until they are sticky and coated. Serve them hot with more barbecue sauce on the side.

LEMONY BAKED HAM

One of the real Laura Ingalls's favorite things to do was to play catch with a blown-up pig's bladder that her Pa would make for her when he was butchering hogs. I'll do that the day pigs can fly. So, instead of instructions on how to make your own pig's bladder ball, I'm including my recipe for baked ham. It's just so much more . . . pleasant. This deceptively simple ham is absolutely delicious.

 Serves 12, with plenty of leftovers

1 (14- to 16-pound/6.3- to 7.2-kg) fully cooked bone-in ham
20 to 30 whole cloves
½ cup (110 g) packed light brown sugar
Grated zest of 2 lemons

- Take the ham out of the refrigerator about 1 hour before you are ready to bake it.

- Preheat the oven to 425°F (220°C).

- Peel off the ham skin, but leave the fat. Make a crisscross pattern across the ham with a sharp knife, creating a diamond pattern. Place the ham in a shallow roasting pan, and stick 2 or 3 whole cloves into each diamond.

- Mix the brown sugar with the lemon zest in a small bowl. Rub it all over the ham. Bake for 20 minutes, then reduce the heat to 350°F (175°C) and bake for about 45 minutes more, until a knife inserted in the middle comes out hot. Let the ham cool slightly before carving.

CHICKEN-FRIED STEAK
WITH CREAM GRAVY

This is possibly the ultimate stick-to-your-ribs prairie dinner. It's also my all-time-favorite, most indulgent, "I don't care in the least about my weight today" meal.

Serves 6

- Make the steaks: Trim any fat from the steaks and, using a mallet or rolling pin, pound out the steaks to ¼ inch (6 mm) thick.

- Beat together the milk and egg in a shallow dish and set aside. Place the flour in another shallow dish, season with the seasoned salt and pepper, and set aside.

- Cover the bottom of a large skillet, preferably cast iron, with enough oil to reach about ½ inch (12 mm).

- Coat the steaks in the egg mixture, then in the flour mixture, and add them to the pan (you will need to do this in batches). Cook until the bottom is nice and brown, 2 to 3 minutes. Flip the steaks and cook for another 2 to 3 minutes. Be careful to not overcook them. Continue this process until all the steaks are cooked, placing the finished steaks on a paper towel–lined baking sheet to drain.

- After frying the steaks, make the cream gravy: Pour off most of the oil, leaving about ¼ cup (60 ml) behind along with all the brown bits. Add the flour, whisking until it is well mixed. Place the skillet back over medium-high heat and slowly add the milk while stirring constantly. Cook until the gravy comes to a boil. Season with salt and pepper. Serve it hot over the chicken-fried steaks.

For the Steaks:

6 (½-inch/12-mm-thick) rib-eye
    steaks (6 ounces/170 g each)
¾ cup (180 ml) milk
1 large egg, beaten
2½ to 3 cups (315 g) all-purpose
    flour
2 teaspoons seasoned salt
1 teaspoon freshly ground black
    pepper
Canola oil for frying

For the Cream Gravy:

3 heaping tablespoons all-purpose
    flour
2 cups (480 ml) milk
Salt and freshly ground black
    pepper

SMOKY SPICY BEEFY CHILI

Southwestern settlers used dried beef for their chili. My (bean-free) chili is made with fresh beef chuck and is great on its own. But here's a fun and contemporary way to serve it at a Super Bowl party, or any party for that matter: Get some individual-size bags of Fritos (the kind for school lunches), put a bag in a bowl, slice the bag open lengthwise, kind of like a baked potato, and spoon chili over the chips inside. Then top with cheese and all the other toppings. Voilà . . . Frito pie.

continued

¼ cup (60 ml) vegetable oil

4 pounds (1.8 kg) well-trimmed
    boneless beef chuck (from
    about 5 pounds/2.3 kg total),
    cut into ½-inch (12-mm) cubes

2 medium onions, chopped

1 head garlic (about 15 cloves),
    chopped

¼ cup (30 g) ground ancho chile
    powder

2 tablespoons ground cumin

½ teaspoon ground allspice

¼ teaspoon ground cinnamon

¼ teaspoon ground cloves

1 (12-ounce/360-ml) bottle dark
    beer

1 (28-ounce/800-g) can diced
    tomatoes, with juice

2 teaspoons dried oregano

2 tablespoons salt, plus more for
    serving

2 tablespoons tomato paste

3 tablespoons masa harina

Coarsely grated sharp Cheddar
    cheese, for serving (optional)

Chopped green and/or red onion,
    for serving (optional)

Chopped fresh cilantro, for serving
    (optional)

Diced fresh tomatoes, for serving
    (optional)

Sour cream, for serving (optional)

- Heat 1 tablespoon of the oil in a large pot over medium-high heat. Add one-third of the beef; sprinkle it with salt. Cook until browned, stirring occasionally, about 3 minutes. Using a slotted spoon, transfer the beef to a large bowl. Repeat two more times with 2 more tablespoons oil and the remaining two batches of beef.

- Reduce the heat to medium. Add the remaining 1 tablespoon oil and the onions. Sauté until soft, 8 to 10 minutes. Add the garlic; cook and stir for 2 minutes. Add the ancho chile powder, cumin, allspice, cinnamon, and cloves; cook and stir for about 1 minute. Add the beer; stir for 1 minute, scraping up the browned bits.

- Return the beef and any accumulated juices to the pot. Add the canned tomatoes with their juice, 2 cups (480 ml) of water, the oregano, and 2 teaspoons of salt. Bring the chili to a boil. Reduce the heat to low, cover it with the lid slightly ajar, and simmer gently until the beef is just tender, 1¾ to 2 hours.

- Let the chili cool for 1 hour, then refrigerate it uncovered until cold. Cover and refrigerate it overnight.

- The next day, spoon the fat from the top of the chili. Bring the chili to a simmer over medium heat. Stir in the tomato paste. Sprinkle the masa harina over the top; stir to blend. Simmer uncovered until thickened and the beef is very tender, stirring often and adding water by ¼ cup (60 ml) at a time if it is too thick, about 30 minutes.

- Divide the chili among bowls. Serve it hot with desired garnishes.

GILBERT FAMILY MEAT LOAF

Everyone should have a family recipe for meat loaf, right? Well, here's mine. You can substitute ground turkey for the beef and pork, if you like. As you would certainly expect with any venerable family meat loaf, this one is also great served cold the next day as a sandwich.

Serves 6

- Preheat the oven to 350°F (175°C) with a rack in middle.

- Soak the bread crumbs in the milk in a large bowl.

- Meanwhile, melt the butter in a large heavy skillet over medium heat and cook the onion, celery, carrot, and garlic, stirring occasionally, for 5 minutes. Cover the skillet and reduce the heat to low, then cook until the carrot is tender, about 5 minutes.

- Remove from the heat and stir in the Worcestershire sauce, vinegar, salt, pepper, and allspice. Add the onion mixture to the bread crumb mixture.

- Add the beef to the onion mixture along with the pork, bacon, eggs, and parsley and mix together with your hands.

- Pack the mixture into a 9-by-5-inch (23-by-12-cm) oval loaf or a 9-by-13-inch (23-by-33-cm) shallow baking dish. Bake until an instant-read thermometer inserted into the center of the meat loaf registers 155°F (70°C), 1 to 1¼ hours. Let it cool for about 5 minutes before serving.

1 cup (55 g) finely ground fresh bread crumbs (from 2 slices firm white bread)
⅓ cup (75 ml) whole milk
2 tablespoons unsalted butter
1 yellow onion, finely chopped
1 celery rib, finely chopped
1 carrot, finely chopped
3 cloves garlic, minced
2 tablespoons Worcestershire sauce
1 tablespoon apple-cider vinegar
2 teaspoons salt
1½ teaspoons freshly ground black pepper
¼ teaspoon ground allspice
1½ pounds (680 g) ground beef chuck
8 ounces (225 g) ground pork
4 ounces (115 g) bacon (about 4 slices), finely chopped
2 large eggs
⅓ cup (10 g) finely chopped fresh parsley

RACK OF LAMB WITH ROSEMARY AND THYME

This special-occasion dish is pretty, elegant, and delightful. Garnish with a few thyme and rosemary sprigs before you take it to the table. It makes a wonderful Easter meal, served with Potatoes au Gratin (page 154) and Minty Peas and Carrots (page 147).

continued

1 (1¾-pound/800-g) rack of lamb

Salt and freshly ground black
    pepper

2 tablespoons olive oil

2 tablespoons chopped fresh
    rosemary

1 tablespoon chopped fresh thyme

10 cloves garlic, smashed

Fresh sprigs thyme and/or
    rosemary, for serving (optional)

- Preheat the oven to 450°F (230°C).

- Season the lamb with salt and pepper. Heat the oil in a 12-inch (30.50-cm) cast-iron skillet over medium-high heat. Add the lamb, fat-side down, and cook, searing the bottom and sides of the rack, until browned, about 10 minutes. Turn the lamb fat-side up in the skillet and scatter the rosemary and thyme over the top. Add the garlic to the skillet and transfer it to the oven.

- Roast until an instant-read thermometer inserted into the center of the meat reads 130°F (55°C) for medium-rare, about 10 minutes. Let it cool for 5 minutes before slicing the rack into portions and serving. Garnish with a few sprigs of thyme and/or rosemary, if desired.

CORNMEAL FRIED CATFISH

This is a prairie dish and it's also a bayou dish. I shot a movie in New Orleans a long time ago. One day we were shooting in the middle of a bayou somewhere when there was a knock on my dressing room door. I opened it, and there was the man on whose property we were filming. He was carrying a huge baking sheet piled high with catfish he'd just caught, cleaned, and fried. I took one bite, and it was so good that I started to cry. I never learned his name, but he was very sweet and gave me his recipe. Here it is.

Serves 8

- Preheat the oven to 200°F (95°C). Pour the oil into a large, deep cast-iron or heavy skillet to a depth of 3 inches (7.5 cm) and heat over medium-high heat until hot, but not smoking.

- Meanwhile, combine the cornmeal, flour, seasoned salt, garlic salt, lemon pepper, cayenne, and black pepper to taste in a large shallow dish. Thoroughly dredge the catfish fillets in the mixture, gently shaking off the excess.

- Working in batches to avoid crowding, fry the catfish in the hot oil, without turning, until golden and crisp, 5 to 6 minutes. Keep the finished pieces warm in the oven while you fry the remaining catfish.

- Transfer the fillets with a slotted spatula to paper towels to drain. Season to taste with salt and serve immediately.

Vegetable oil, for frying
1 cup (160 g) yellow cornmeal
½ cup (60 g) all-purpose flour
3 tablespoons seasoned salt
1 tablespoon garlic salt
½ teaspoon lemon pepper
¼ teaspoon cayenne pepper
Freshly ground black pepper
3½ pounds (1.6 kg) catfish fillets, cut into 8 equal pieces
Salt

PAN-FRIED TROUT
WITH BUTTER SAUCE

I sure did a lot of fishing on *Little House*. I also love to fish for real—only if someone else will actually clean the fish, though. I'm fine with baiting hooks and so forth. I'm just not very good at handling fish innards. I actually created this recipe after a productive day of fishing with my boys.

Serves 4

- Preheat the oven to 200°F (90°C).

- Melt 2 tablespoons of the butter in a 12-inch (30.5-cm) heavy skillet (preferably oval) over low heat, and then remove it from the heat.

- Rinse the trout and pat them dry. Brush with the melted butter inside and out and season with ¾ teaspoon of the salt. Mound the flour on a sheet of wax paper, then dredge each fish in the flour to coat completely, shaking off any excess.

- Add the oil and 2 more tablespoons of the butter to the skillet over medium-high heat until the foam subsides, then sauté the trout (in two batches if necessary), gently turning them over once using spatulas, until golden brown and almost cooked through, about 7 minutes total (the fish will continue to cook as it stands). Transfer each trout to a plate and keep it warm in the oven.

- Pour off the fat from the skillet and wipe the skillet clean. Melt the remaining ¼ cup (½ stick/55 g) of butter over medium-low heat. Add the parsley, pepper, and remaining ¼ teaspoon of salt, swirling the skillet to combine, and remove it from the heat. Add the lemon juice, swirling the skillet to incorporate. Spoon the sauce over the trout and serve them immediately with lemon wedges.

½ cup (1 stick/115 g) unsalted butter
4 (8-ounce/225-g) whole brook, rainbow, or brown trout, cleaned, head and tail intact
1 teaspoon salt
¾ cup (90 g) all-purpose flour
3 tablespoons vegetable oil
2 tablespoons chopped fresh parsley
¼ teaspoon freshly ground black pepper
1 tablespoon freshly squeezed lemon juice
Lemon wedges, for serving

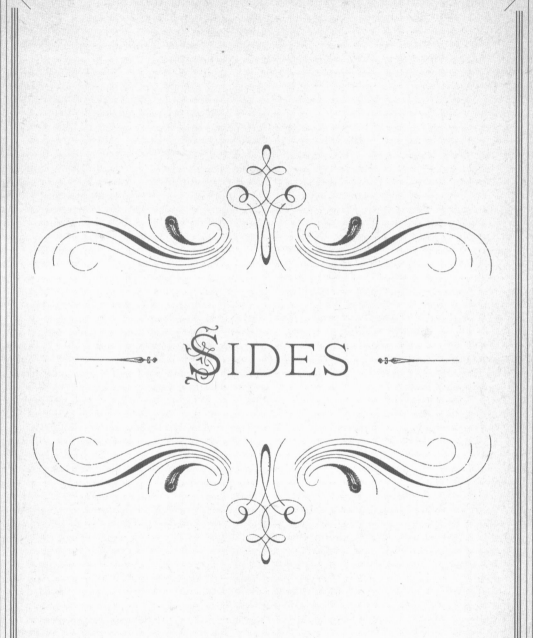

SIDES

LITTLE HOUSE
BLOOPERS AND GOOFS

Let me start by saying that there was no way for us to stick strictly to the *Little House* books. If we had done that, there would have been only nine episodes of the show, instead of the hundreds we filmed over nine seasons. The producers took a great deal of dramatic license by adding characters and situations that didn't exist or happen in the books. For example, the Ingalls family moved *a lot* in real life. They did not live out the majority of their years in Walnut Grove.

And for the record, there was no Albert Ingalls in real life. Nor was there a James or a Cassandra Ingalls. Mary Ingalls never married in real life, therefore there was no Adam Kendall, nor was there a baby boy who died in a fire. I could go on and on with this list, but if you have read the books, you know what's what. And this book is about the TV series, after all.

That, however, doesn't let us off the hook for some pretty glaring and hilarious bloopers and goofs. Here are a few courtesy of Lennon Parker at the PrairieFans.com web site, with additional commentary from yours truly:

1. Laura must have carried her baby, Rose, for more than a year. In the season seven episode "I Do, Again," Laura announces she's pregnant, and it's warm enough for Charles and Almanzo to be working outside without coats. Then in "A Wiser Heart," a pregnant Laura (who isn't even showing yet) goes to Arizona to attend a seminar with Eliza Jane over the summer when they're off from school. In the episode "A Christmas They Never Forgot," Laura is really showing, and in the episode "Stone Soup," a very pregnant Laura suffers heatstroke while trying to water the apple orchard during a drought, which means it must have been late spring or summer again.

   My take: I had never noticed this before. *Hmmm* . . . nothing was ever easy back in those days! My first baby, Dakota, was two weeks late. I was miserable. Poor Laura, pregnant for more than a year!

2. In the episode "His Father's Son," John Jr. finds out that Isaiah can't read. At the end of the episode, we see Isaiah up in the tree house with a McGuffey Reader, starting the process of learning. Then in "To Live with Fear," which is several episodes later, Isaiah picks up a telegram from Charles and Caroline about Mary's condition, and when Grace asks him what it says, he shakes his head to indicate that he can't read it. I thought it was a little strange that he forgot how to read!

   My take: This is a nice catch. Maybe all that spitting made him forget? Or perhaps he was swigging that moonshine again?

3. In the season five episode "The Cheaters," Andrew asks his mom to walk home with him after school. Mrs. Garvey says to Andrew, "I can't right now, I need to stop at the grocery store." She slipped up and called it a grocery store instead of the Mercantile! (The word *groceries* didn't become common until after 1913, when an American firm copyrighted the word *groceteria*.)

   My take: Yes, and if you listen to the school kids in the background, you can hear some saying "Right on!" and "All right!" What can I say? We tried, but sometimes the 1970s slipped into the 1870s.

4. Almanzo didn't call Laura "Bess" in the books, but he called her that in real life. So why was her nickname "Beth" on the TV show? Maybe Michael Landon thought Melissa Gilbert seemed more like a Beth than a Bess, or maybe they thought "Beth" would be easier for viewers to hear.

    My take: I have no idea. Nor did I ever ask. Beth, Bess—they kind of sound the same. I don't know why the producers would have changed the nickname. And I have no idea why Almanzo called Laura "Bess" in the first place. Her middle name was Elizabeth, so Beth makes more sense than Bess—unless Almanzo had a lisp.

5. Whatever happened to Doc Baker's assistant, Dr. Caleb Ledoux? He appeared in one episode, "Dark Sage," in season eight as a black doctor working for Doc Baker. He faced the skepticism and prejudice of the town until he saved a pregnant woman's life, and at the end of the episode, the townspeople convince him to stay on in Walnut Grove. Where'd he go?

    My take: We had a lot of characters who popped into town and then up and disappeared. But if we'd kept everyone who moved to Walnut Grove on the show, the final episode would have been six hours long instead of two.

6. In "Bless All the Dear Children," Laura's baby, Rose, is kidnapped. It was Christmastime and in Minnesota it would have been extremely cold. But not one person is wearing a jacket and there is no snow to be seen! I'm not saying that it snows every year for Christmas, but at least it should have been cold.

    My take: That is because we shot it in old Tucson over the summer—misery personified. And, might I add, this is my least favorite performance of my own during the run of the show. I really phoned this one in. I'm not sure why, but I just couldn't connect to this particular story. Maybe it's because I wasn't a parent yet. All I know is that I was in way over my head in this one, and I was really sweaty too!

7. In season three's "Little Girl Lost" episode, Mary is shown closing the cabinet in the kitchen. Then the camera focuses on Laura and the cabinet is still open, and it's even open a little while later when they leave.

    My take: It's those haunted prairie cabinets. Or maybe it was the Creeper of Walnut Grove!

8. In the first episode of season nine, called "Times are Changing," Almanzo says he hasn't seen his brother Royal in more than ten years. But didn't he show up in the season seven episode "The Nephews"? Had ten years elapsed between season seven and season nine? Wow, they aged nicely! And whatever happened to the nephews? When Royal shows up with Jenny, the nephews aren't even mentioned. It was also funny when Laura said it was nice to finally meet both of them, after she had already met Royal. When Royal tells them Jenny has no other family, you have to wonder what happened to the boys who supposedly grew up to be a preacher and a doctor.

    My take: Okay, here's an example of dramatic license gone horribly awry. Remember when I said earlier that some characters pop into Walnut Grove and then disappear? Well, that is exactly what happened here. I don't know why the boys came to visit! And I don't know where they disappeared to! I don't know why Royal came back! I'm just a puppet, a slave to the whim and will of the show's creators.

9. In the season five episode "The Enchanted Cottage," Mrs. Oleson talks to Mrs. Foster and calls her Matilda. But in the episode "Stone Soup," Harriet calls her Anne, and in "If I Should Wake Before I Die," she is called Ruth. It's strange how many names she's been called in this series.

    My take: The actress's real name is Ruth Foster. I'm not sure what exactly happened here myself. Perhaps Mrs. Foster has multiple personalities. Or maybe Mrs. Oleson never really learned her name. I'm fresh out of excuses.

10. In the season four episode "Freedom Flight," there's a big but very funny blooper: After MacGregor and the others find out that Charles is hiding the Indians at his place, a scene follows where Charles and Doc Baker drive the Indians away to get them to safety. Then a hand appears at the bottom right of the screen. It is the person who was shaking the wagon for the camera! He is even wearing a watch!

    My take: Sure, all wagons back in the 1800s came with a shaker who wore one of them newfangled timepieces!

11. In the season nine episode "Home Again," Laura comes by the house and Charles pours her a cup of coffee. In previous episodes, when they pour coffee, they have a cloth around the handle to keep from burning their hands. In this episode, Charles just picks the pot up with no cloth on the handle.

    My take: He had asbestos hands. He was impervious to pain or heat. He was Super Pa! I don't know! These bloopers are starting to hurt my head.

12. In the season one episode "Plague," Charles goes to Eric's house, and he finds him sitting underneath a tree. While he's telling Charles about what a great day it is for his son to be out of school, the boy's fingers twitch. Twice. And his eyelids flutter. Very strange, since the boy is supposed to be dead.

    My take: The living dead, apparently. We were *waaaay* ahead of our time with the zombie theme.

13. At the end of the season eight episode "A Wiser Heart," Laura asks for a train ticket to Walnut Grove. Since when did the train go to Walnut Grove? The closest connection was Sleepy Eye or Mankato.

    My take: Oh, just cut it out, will ya?! Some people are so picky . . . and so right!

14. In the season nine episode "Rage," when Laura takes Rose from Mr. Stark, you can see that he is holding a doll. You can see blond doll hair peeking through the blanket.

    My take: Would you let that man hold a real baby?! He was out of control. Perhaps Laura was being extra sneaky. Okay, okay, you caught us using a doll instead of the real baby—we did that a lot. Especially when the babies were wrapped for the day or we were doing something dangerous like letting a crazy man hold a baby while waving a gun and knocking over a kerosene lamp. In all seriousness, working with Robert Loggia was a joy and an honor. He remains a friend to this day.

15. In the season two episode "Remember Me," Mary and Laura jump into the water to save some puppies from drowning. When they jump in, they're both wearing their shoes and stockings. When they are swimming, both of them are barefoot. And when they get out of the water, they have their shoes and stockings back on again!

    My take: Yes. Those are my magic shoes. No, wait, that's from *Forrest Gump*. Actually, this is a pure and simple continuity mistake, sorry.

16. At the end of the season two episode "For My Lady," Laura says that Ma uses the dishes that Pa gave her every day because special dishes aren't for special occasions but for special people. Nice sentiment, but we never see those dishes again!

    My take: Yes. That's because I sold the dishes to get Ma a stove . . . wait . . . I sold my pony to get the stove, so maybe the dishes broke in a tornado or a hailstorm, or maybe the raccoon broke them. Actually, I think everyone forgot about them. Oh well.

17. In season one, Laura trades her horse, Bunny, to Nellie in exchange for a stove from the Mercantile. We don't see or hear about Bunny until season three. What happened to Bunny during all of season two?

    My take: Bunny was very busy pulling a stagecoach filled with all of the made-up characters.

18. At the end of the season nine episode "Home Again," where Albert kicks his morphine addiction, Laura tells the audience that Albert comes back to Walnut Grove years later as a doctor. But at the end of "Look Back to Yesterday," it's implied that his death is imminent. Does he come back as a doctor or does he die?

    My take: Ah yes, this is a tricky one. Albert did come back—as a zombie doctor. Okay, he wasn't a zombie, though that would have been a fun twist. This is one of the great glaring mistakes the creators of the show made. But let's be honest—would any of you love *Little House* less without this blooper? Isn't it bloopers like these (and the hunt for them) that are among the things that make *Little House* so endearing in the first place?

19. In the season five episode "The Odyssey," a vagrant tries to throw Albert off the train and ends up being pushed out by Laura. But the dummy that is actually tossed from the train can be seen sitting upright in the grass as the stuntman rolls down the hill from the spot the dummy landed.

    My take: I could do a whole riff on dummies and stuntmen and actors, but I'm just going to leave this one alone.

20. In the episode from season one called "Country Girls," Charles and Caroline don't bother to take the girls to their first day of school after settling down in Walnut Grove. Yet in "Here Come the Brides," Luke has his father take him to school on his very first day.

    My take: That's because Laura and Mary were very brave and Luke was a big scaredy-cat! And who is Luke anyway? Oh yeah, one of those made-up characters that pops in and then disappears. If I were Luke, I'd be scared too!

21. Weren't these folks some of the cleanest dirt farmers you ever saw?

    My take: Now really, would anyone have watched if we were all dirty and disheveled? Also, we all would have had really rotten teeth—not pretty!

22. In the season eight episode "Wave of the Future," Mrs. Oleson turns Nellie's restaurant into a "Mrs. Sullivan's." In order to get her out of a bad franchise contract, Charles and Nels open a competing restaurant, which puts her out of business. At the end, Colonel Sanders shows up to offer a deal to Harriet to start a chicken-only franchise, but Colonel Sanders wasn't even *born* yet in the 1880s. (And Kentucky Fried Chicken wasn't founded until 1952.)

    My take: I'm telling you, dramatic license is a very powerful thing. It can cause people to be born nearly a century early! When I got this script I thought, "Huh? Colonel Sanders lived in the 1800s?" Looking back, I see that the Colonel Sanders appearance is ridiculous, but that's what makes it kind of fun too.

Okay, I am going to end this section by addressing one of the most frequently asked questions and one of the most frequently pointed-out bloopers. In the season six episode "May We Make Them Proud," Albert accidentally sets the blind school on fire, and Mrs. Garvey and Mary's baby are trapped inside. People ask all the time, "Why did Mrs. Garvey use Mary's baby as a battering ram against the window to try to escape the fire?"

Here's my final word on the subject: There was no Mrs. Garvey. Mary Ingalls never married, so there could never have been a baby. There was no Albert to start the fire in the blind school that didn't really exist. (Did you ever notice how much the school for the blind looks like the Keller house in the version of *The Miracle Worker* I did in 1980?)

It was all made up! All of it, from whole cloth.

All things being equal, let's assume that it all was real and it all happened. If you look really, really closely, you can see that Mrs. Garvey is using her own arm and elbow to try to break the glass. Yes, it's the arm that's holding the baby, but it's still her own arm. It's a really scary moment—acted perfectly, in my opinion. It never even occurred to me that she had used the baby to break the window. Not until all of you started asking me about it!

So, the bottom line is NO. Made-up Mrs. Garvey did not use Mary's made-up baby as a battering ram to break the window of the burning made-up school for the blind!

CUCUMBER-DILL SALAD

This cool, crisp salad is so refreshing on warm days. It's great with MG's Barbecued Ribs (page 112), burgers, or anything, really. Make it with regular cucumbers or the smaller Kirby cucumbers.

Serves 8

- Place the cucumber slices on a flat plate. Salt them lightly and tilt the plate so that excess water will drain off easily. Let them stand for about 1 hour.

- Pass the garlic cloves through a garlic press into a small bowl. Add the yogurt, dill, lemon juice, and salt and white pepper to taste; stir until well mixed. Add the oil and stir vigorously until blended.

- Place the drained cucumber slices in a salad bowl, add the onion (if using), pour the dressing over the top, and toss gently. Refrigerate for about 1 hour, then serve.

4 cucumbers, peeled and thinly sliced
Salt
3 cloves garlic
⅔ cup (165 ml) plain yogurt
2 tablespoons minced fresh dill
1 tablespoon freshly squeezed lemon juice
Freshly ground white pepper
3 tablespoons extra-virgin olive oil
½ Maui onion, very thinly sliced (optional)

CORN AND VIDALIA ONION SALAD

It seems that we were always fretting over the crops on *Little House*: wheat or corn, corn or wheat. And rightly so. To this day, corn remains one of the United States' primary crops. It's also incredibly delicious and full of vitamins and minerals. This salad is really good made with any corn, but it's just a step above magnificent if you make it with fresh sweet white corn. As I write this recipe, I can still hear my firstborn son at age two seeing this salad on the table and screaming at the top of his lungs, "Yay Corneeeeeeeeeyyyyyyy!"

 *Serves 6*

4 ears corn, shucked
Cooking spray
1 large Vidalia onion, cut into
    ½-inch-thick (12-mm) slices
1¼ cups (40 g) finely chopped
    fresh cilantro
1¼ cups (230 g) seeded chopped
    yellow tomato
3 tablespoons rice vinegar
½ teaspoon salt
½ teaspoon freshly ground black
    pepper
¼ teaspoon red pepper flakes

- Prepare a charcoal or gas grill for level heat or preheat the broiler.

- Place the corn on the grill or in a broiler pan. Cook for 20 minutes, until lightly browned all over, turning every 5 minutes. Let it cool, then cut the kernels from the ears (you should have about 3 cups/450 g).

- Coat the grill or broiler pan with cooking spray. Grill the onion slices for 5 minutes on each side.

- Combine the corn, onion, and all remaining ingredients in a large bowl. Toss well and serve.

GREENY McGREEN GREEN SALAD

The secret of this salad is the dressing. There's something about it that magically makes raw vegetables appealing to anyone . . . even children! Use your imagination here; add any and all green veggies that you like: green peppers, zucchini, arugula, kale, and so forth. Just keep it green, otherwise you'll have to change the name. For example, if you add carrots it would have to be "Greeny McGreen Green and a Little Orange Salad."

 Serves 4 to 6

3 tablespoons olive oil

1½ tablespoons freshly squeezed
    lemon juice

1 teaspoon honey or maple syrup

1 teaspoon Dijon mustard

2 heads romaine lettuce, torn into
    bite-size pieces

1 large cucumber, peeled and
    sliced

2 ribs celery, chopped

1 bunch scallions, chopped

- Mix together the oil, lemon juice, honey, and mustard in a large bowl. Add all of the veggies and toss. Serve immediately.

SWEET-AND-SOUR SOUTHERN GREEN BEANS

This recipe comes courtesy of my best friend, Sandy Peckinpah. It's her grandmother's recipe. I never serve my General Gilbert's California Fried Chicken with Pan Gravy (page 96) without also serving these green beans.

Serves 4

- Cook the green beans in boiling water until soft, about 7 minutes. Drain and set aside.

- Cook the bacon in a large frying pan over medium heat until crisp. Drain it on paper towels. Sauté the onion in the bacon fat until soft and golden, 5 to 7 minutes.

- Mix the vinegar and sugar in a small bowl. Add them to the onion in the pan and simmer for 10 minutes. Add the green beans to the onion mixture. Crumble the cooked bacon and stir it into the green bean mixture. Season with salt and pepper to taste. Bring everything to a boil, then reduce the heat to very low and simmer gently, covered, for about 45 minutes. Serve warm.

1 pound (455 g) green beans
4 slices bacon
1 red onion, sliced
½ cup (120 ml) apple-cider vinegar
½ cup (100 g) granulated sugar
Salt and freshly ground black
    pepper

BROCCOLI-CHEDDAR BAKE

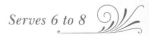

This homey family-style dish is yet another way to make veggie haters learn to love their vegetables. It's amazing what cheese can do. If you like, substitute cauliflower for the broccoli or equal parts Gruyère and Parmesan for the Cheddar.

Serves 6 to 8

- Preheat the oven to 375°F (190°C). Grease a 9-by-13-inch (23-by-33-cm) baking dish.

- In a large bowl, combine the flour, milk, eggs, butter, baking powder, salt, and pepper and mix well to combine.

- Add the broccoli and onion to the bowl and mix. Add the cheese and stir to blend.

- Pour the mixture into the prepared baking dish and bake, covered, for 60 to 75 minutes, until set and golden brown on top. Let it cool for a few minutes before serving.

2 cups (250 g) all-purpose flour

2 cups (480 ml) milk

4 large eggs

⅔ cup (150 g) unsalted butter, melted

2 teaspoons baking powder

2 teaspoons salt

1 teaspoon freshly black ground pepper

3 large bunches broccoli, finely chopped (with stems, if desired)

1 yellow onion, minced or grated

1 pound (455 g) Cheddar cheese, shredded

SAUTÉED BRUSSELS SPROUTS WITH BREAD CRUMBS

I make this dish every few weeks. It's a big favorite at my house. I was quite surprised by everyone's reactions the first time I served it, but the mystery was solved after I tasted it myself. It's an absolute winner!

 Serves 4 to 6

Salt
2 pounds (910 g) Brussels sprouts, trimmed
¼ cup (½ stick/55 g) unsalted butter
1 clove garlic, crushed
¼ cup (30 g) dry bread crumbs
2 tablespoons freshly squeezed lemon juice
Salt and freshly ground black pepper

- Bring a large pot of salted water to a boil over high heat. Add the Brussels sprouts and boil until just about cooked through, 3 to 5 minutes. Drain them in a colander and rinse under cold running water to stop them from cooking any further. Cut them in half lengthwise.

- Melt the butter in a large heavy-bottomed skillet over medium heat. Add the garlic and cook until the edges begin to brown, about 2 minutes, then remove and discard the garlic. Add the Brussels sprouts to the skillet, increase the heat to high, and cook, stirring often, until the sprouts are well browned in places, about 5 minutes. Sprinkle the bread crumbs over the sprouts and stir well, then add the lemon juice and stir. Season to taste with salt and pepper and serve hot.

ASIAN GLAZED CARROTS

Anyone can make glazed carrots—I bet Ma Ingalls did—but these are my own Asian-style glazed carrots. Their flavor is complex but they're still easy to make. By this point, you can see that I've worked hard to create different ways to get my kids to eat vegetables. They love this carrot dish so much that I have to triple it every time.

Serves 4

- Heat the oil in a large skillet over medium-high heat. Add the carrots and cook until limp, 2 to 3 minutes. Add the sake, soy sauce, and sugar. Cook until the liquid evaporates, 4 to 6 minutes. Stir in the red pepper and serve hot.

3 tablespoons vegetable oil
4 carrots, peeled and julienned
¼ cup (60 ml) sake
¼ cup (60 ml) soy sauce
2 tablespoons granulated sugar
¼ teaspoon red pepper flakes

MINTY PEAS AND CARROTS

This dish is very simple and very delicate, and the mint makes it unexpected and refreshing. I like to serve it with the Rack of Lamb with Rosemary and Thyme (page 120) or the Lemony Baked Ham (page 114).

Serves 4

- Heat the oil in a large skillet over medium heat. Add the carrots and shallots and cook, stirring, until the carrots are just tender, about 8 minutes. Add the peas and cook, stirring, until heated through, about 3 minutes. Remove the peas and carrots from the heat and stir in the mint and butter. Season to taste with salt and pepper and serve hot.

1 tablespoon olive oil
4 carrots, diced to ½ inch (12 mm)
2 large shallots, halved and thinly sliced
1 pound (455 g) frozen baby peas, thawed
2 tablespoons thinly sliced fresh mint leaves
1¼ tablespoons unsalted butter
Salt and freshly ground black pepper

MIKEY B'S FAVORITE
FRIED CORN

This is my youngest son's favorite way to eat corn on the cob. There's no need for butter or anything else, really, except maybe a touch of salt. This corn makes a great summer meal with MG's Barbecued Ribs (page 112).

Serves 4 to 8

- Pour the oil into a large pot to a depth of 2 inches (5 cm) and heat over medium-high heat until a drop of water sizzles.

- Shuck the corn, removing all of the silk, and fry it, several ears at a time, until most of the kernels are deep golden, 3 to 4 minutes per batch. Drain the corn on paper towels and season to taste with salt. Serve immediately.

Vegetable oil, for frying
8 ears supersweet corn
Salt

CREAMED SPINACH WITH BACON AND SHALLOTS

Want your young ones to eat their spinach? Serve this dish and watch it disappear! In fact, I always double this one. Try it alongside the Pan-Fried Trout with Butter Sauce (page 125).

Serves 6

3 pounds (1.4 kg) spinach, stems trimmed
¾ cup (1½ sticks/170 g) unsalted butter
¼ cup (30 g) all-purpose flour
¾ cup (180 ml) milk
8 slices bacon, finely chopped
3 shallots, finely chopped
¾ cup (180 ml) heavy cream
Salt and freshly ground black pepper

- Bring a large pot of water to a boil over high heat. Add the spinach and cook until the leaves are completely wilted, 30 to 40 seconds. Drain the spinach in a colander set in the sink and cool under cold running water. Using your hands, squeeze out as much excess water as possible from the spinach. Transfer the spinach to a cutting board, chop, and set it aside.

- Melt ½ cup (1 stick/115 g) of the butter in a medium saucepan over medium heat. Add the flour and whisk for 2 minutes. Gradually whisk in the milk, then stir constantly with a wooden spoon until the mixture is thick and pasty, 2 to 3 minutes. Remove the pan from the heat.

- Melt 2 more tablespoons of the butter in a large skillet over medium heat. Add the bacon and fry, stirring often, until it begins to brown, about 5 minutes. Add the shallots and fry, stirring often, until the bacon is golden brown, 3 to 4 minutes more. Stir in the spinach. Add the milk mixture and stir until melted and incorporated. Add the cream and the remaining 2 tablespoons of butter, season to taste with salt and pepper, and cook until thickened, 1 to 2 minutes more. Serve immediately.

ZUCCHINI FRITTERS

By now you're probably wondering, "Where is the fritter recipe? This is a prairie cookbook! How could she not include a fritter recipe?" Well, calm down—here it is, although it might not be the fritter recipe you were expecting. I promise you'll love it, though; it's excellent served with salsa and sour cream. So don't get yourself all atwitter. Please try this fritter. Though it's not sweet, it's certainly not bitter. There now . . . isn't that better?

Serves 4

- Heat 2 tablespoons of the oil in a medium nonstick skillet over medium heat. Add the onions and cook, stirring frequently with a wooden spoon, until soft, about 5 minutes. Set aside and let them cool.

- Grate the zucchini on the large holes of a box grater. Working in batches, put a small mound of zucchini in the center of a large square of double-layer cheesecloth. Gather the corners together and squeeze out as much water as possible. Transfer the zucchini to a medium bowl. Repeat with the remaining zucchini.

- Add the onions, egg, and flour to the zucchini, season with salt and pepper, and mix well with a spoon until thoroughly combined.

- Heat the remaining 4 tablespoons (60 ml) of oil in the same skillet over medium heat. Gently form the zucchini mixture into 8 patties about ¾ inch (2 cm) thick. Working in batches, fry the patties in the hot oil until browned and crisp, 2 to 3 minutes per side.

- Transfer the fritters with a slotted spatula to paper towels to drain and season with salt while still hot. Serve immediately.

6 tablespoons (90 ml) corn oil
2 yellow onions, finely chopped
4 zucchini, ends trimmed
1 large egg, lightly beaten
2 tablespoons all-purpose flour
Salt and freshly ground black
    pepper

POTATOES AU GRATIN

One of the all-time great side dishes. This rich version is closer to the authentic French dish than some other recipes you might see. It's absolutely fantastic with steak or lamb, or even swordfish. I have to hide the finished gratin until I'm ready to serve or else my family will pass through the kitchen and sneak bites. Okay . . . so do I . . . you caught me.

 *Serves 6*

5 tablespoons (70 g) unsalted
    butter
2 cloves garlic
Salt
6 large russet potatoes (about
    2½ pounds/1.2 kg), peeled
    and thinly sliced (about ⅛ inch/
    3 mm thick)
2 cups (480 ml) half-and-half
Freshly ground black pepper
Pinch of ground nutmeg
1 cup grated Gruyère cheese
    (about 4 ounces/115 g)

- Preheat the oven to 400°F (205°C). Grease an 8-inch (20-cm) square baking dish with 1 tablespoon of the butter.

- Smash the garlic with the side of a knife and sprinkle it generously with salt. Chop and scrape the garlic into a mushy paste.

- Cut the remaining 4 tablespoons (½ stick/55 g) butter into ½-inch (12-mm) pieces. Combine the garlic paste, potatoes, half-and-half, and butter in a large pot; stir. Season with salt and a few turns of the pepper mill and taste the liquid; it should be seasoned generously. Add the nutmeg. Bring everything to a boil over medium-high heat while stirring the mixture with a wooden spoon. After 8 to 10 minutes, the potatoes will be a little tender and their starch will have thickened the liquid a lot.

- Transfer the mixture to the prepared baking dish; smooth the top as much as possible. Cover the gratin with the grated cheese and bake until deeply golden brown, 20 to 30 minutes. Let it cool and set a little before serving.

CANDIED YAMS

This not-too-sweet version of this classic dish goes great with my Roast Turkey with Herb Butter (page 104) or any of my chicken dishes. It's also kind of a cool meal all on its own. Or try it for breakfast!

Serves 4 to 6

- Preheat the oven to 375°F (190°C).

- Put the potatoes in a medium baking dish in a single layer.

- Whisk the juice, syrup, ginger, and salt to taste together in a small bowl until smooth, then pour over the potatoes. Cut the butter into small pieces and scatter over the sweet potatoes.

- Bake, basting occasionally with the liquid in the dish, until the potatoes are soft and golden, 1 to 1½ hours. Serve hot.

4 large sweet potatoes, peeled and quartered
1½ cups (360 ml) freshly squeezed orange juice
½ cup (120 ml) maple syrup
1½ teaspoons ground ginger
Salt
¼ cup (½ stick/55 g) unsalted butter

BEST STUFFING EVER

I love stuffing. I always have. It's one of my favorite things to eat—hot, cold, with gravy, or naked (the stuffing, silly). I can't say enough about stuffing. Really! I thought of so many superlatives for this recipe that I had to share a few with you:

- Stuffing for President!
- And the Oscar goes to . . . stuffing!
- World War III ends as entire planet eats stuffing!
- Brad Pitt to marry Melissa Gilbert's stuffing recipe!
- Scientists discover that stuffing cures the common cold!
- Stuffing wins Super Bowl!

Guess what my answer always is to the question, "Stuffing or Potatoes?"

 Serves 6 to 8

15 tablespoons (200 g) unsalted butter
6 ribs celery, finely chopped
2 yellow onions, finely chopped
1 dried bay leaf
Salt and freshly ground black pepper
1 tablespoon finely chopped fresh sage
2 teaspoons finely chopped fresh marjoram
2 teaspoons finely chopped fresh savory
2 teaspoons finely chopped fresh thyme
½ teaspoon ground nutmeg
10 cups (500 g) cubed crustless white bread
3 cups (720 ml) chicken broth
½ cup (15 g) finely chopped fresh parsley
2 large eggs, beaten

- Preheat the oven to 400°F (205°C). Grease a 9-by-13-inch (23-by-33-cm) baking dish with 1 tablespoon of the butter.

- Heat 10 tablespoons (140 g) of the butter in a large skillet over medium-high heat. Add the celery, onions, bay leaf, and salt and pepper to taste; cook until golden brown, 18 to 20 minutes. Add the sage, marjoram, savory, thyme, and nutmeg and cook for about 2 minutes. Discard the bay leaf.

- Transfer the onion mixture to a large bowl. Add the cubed bread, broth, and parsley and season with salt and pepper to taste. Add the eggs and mix to combine.

- Cut the remaining 4 tablespoons (½ stick/55 g) butter into small pieces. Transfer the mixture to the prepared dish, press down, and dot with the butter. Cover with aluminum foil and bake for 30 minutes. Uncover and continue baking until the stuffing is deep golden brown on top, about 20 minutes more. Serve hot.

DIFFERENT-EVERY-TIME BAKED BEANS

<hr>

Baked beans from scratch, although traditional, can take a really long time. There's all that rinsing, soaking, and draining—and waiting. I prefer to take advantage of the modern convenience of canned baked beans. Besides, it's really fun to mix up the different flavors that are out there. You can use any flavors you like. Mix it up each time, and the dish will always be different but just as yummy!

Serves 6 to 8

- Preheat the oven to 350°F (175°C).

- Mix the beans, ketchup, mustard, and barbecue sauce in a large bowl. Pour them into a 9-by-13-inch (23-by-33-cm) baking pan. Cross the bacon slices on top. Bake for 45 minutes, until bubbly. Serve hot.

3 (15-ounce/430-g) cans assorted
 flavor baked beans
½ cup (120 ml) ketchup
½ cup (120 ml) yellow or brown
 mustard
½ cup (120 ml) barbecue sauce
2 slices bacon

CORN BREAD WITH SCALLIONS

One of the staple foods on *Little House* was corn bread. You'll see Ma taking it out of the oven often. You'll see it in picnic scenes, dinner scenes, and even in our lunch pails for school. This corn bread is great with anything, and especially with my Smoky Spicy Beefy Chili (page 117). Be sure to serve this with butter, but bring the butter to room temperature first. That'll keep the corn bread from falling apart when you spread it.

Serves 8

- Preheat the oven to 400°F (205°C). Place a 10-inch (25-cm) cast-iron skillet in the oven to heat.

- In a medium bowl, whisk together the flour, cornmeal, baking powder, salt, and pepper. In a small bowl, whisk together the milk, honey, eggs, and ⅓ cup (75 ml) of the oil. Add the wet ingredients to the cornmeal mixture and whisk just until combined. Stir in the scallions.

- Add the remaining 1 tablespoon of oil to the hot skillet and swirl to coat. Pour the batter into the hot skillet and bake for about 30 minutes, until the top is golden and a toothpick inserted in the center comes out clean. Let it cool slightly, then invert the skillet and turn the corn bread out onto a wire rack to cool. Alternatively, serve the corn bread hot directly from the skillet.

1⅓ cups (165 g) all-purpose flour
1 cup (140 g) coarse stone-ground yellow cornmeal
2 teaspoons baking powder
1 teaspoon salt
Pinch of freshly ground black pepper
1¼ cups (300 ml) low-fat milk
2 tablespoons honey
2 large eggs, beaten
⅓ cup plus 1 tablespoon (90 ml) corn oil
8 scallions (white and tender green parts only), thinly sliced

POPOVERS

Who doesn't love popovers? They are the epitome of light, fluffy, yummy goodness. We didn't eat popovers on *Little House*, but we definitely eat them in my own Little House. Slather these with butter and, if you like, lots of jelly or honey.

 *continued*

Vegetable oil or shortening, for
    popover tins
3 large eggs, at room temperature
1¼ cups (300 ml) milk, at room
    temperature
1¼ cups (155 g) all-purpose flour
Pinch of salt

- Preheat the oven to 450°F (230°C). Oil every other cup (to prevent the popovers from touching each other when they rise) in two 12-cup popover or muffin pans lightly but well.

- Whisk the eggs until lemon-colored and foamy. Add the milk and stir in until well blended. Don't overbeat. Add the flour and salt all at once. Beat by hand until foamy and smooth on top.

- Pour the batter into a pitcher and fill the oiled cups in the pan with batter. Bake for 15 minutes, then reduce the heat to 350°F (175°C) and bake for 30 minutes longer. Don't open the oven door to check or they'll fall!

- Remove the popovers from the pan with a sharp knife, being careful not to pierce them, and serve immediately.

CLASSIC DINNER ROLLS

What's yummier with a great roast dinner than light and fluffy dinner rolls? Now, don't get me wrong—I am a big fan of biscuits. And biscuits are indisputable prairie food (as well as homemade bread). I've just always loved going out to dinner and breaking into a warm, crusty roll with a soft, light center. I adore a simple Parker House dinner roll. I spent years testing and experimenting with different recipes until one day—voilà—I had come as close as possible to the originals. I always have to double this recipe so that there are some for the next day.

- Stir together the milk, yeast, and malt syrup in a large bowl; let it sit until foamy, 10 minutes.

- In a medium bowl, whisk together the flour and salt; add them to the milk mixture along with the softened butter and stir with a wooden spoon until a dough forms. Transfer to a lightly floured work surface and knead until smooth, about 5 minutes. Transfer the dough to a lightly greased bowl and cover with plastic wrap; let it sit in a warm spot until nearly doubled in size, about 1 hour.

- Uncover and punch down the dough; cover again and let rise until puffed and nearly doubled in size, about 45 minutes.

- Preheat the oven to 325°F (165°C). Grease an 8-inch (20-cm) cast-iron skillet or an 8-inch (20-cm) square baking pan.

- Portion the dough into fourteen 1½-inch (4-cm) diameter balls, about 1¼ ounces (35 g) each, and transfer them to the prepared skillet or pan, nestling them side by side; cover loosely with plastic wrap and let them rise in a warm spot until doubled in size, about 2 hours.

- Brush the rolls with the clarified butter and bake for 20 to 22 minutes, until puffed and pale golden brown. Transfer them to a rack and brush with more clarified butter, then sprinkle each roll with a small pinch of sea salt. Serve warm.

¾ cup milk (180 ml), heated to 115°F (45°C)

1 teaspoon active dry yeast

1 teaspoon barley malt syrup or dark corn syrup

2 cups (250 g) all-purpose flour, plus more for dusting

1½ teaspoons kosher salt

2½ tablespoons unsalted butter, cut into ½-inch (12-mm) cubes, softened

¼ cup (½ stick/55 g) clarified butter, for greasing and brushing (see Note)

Sea salt, for serving

NOTE:

To make clarified butter, place the butter in a saucepan over very low heat and let it melt without stirring it. It will separate into foam, liquid, and solids. Skim the foam from the top and discard. Carefully spoon the liquid (your clarified butter) into a clean container. Discard the solids at the bottom. You lose a little volume when you do this, so start out with 5 tablespoons (70 g) to end up with the ¼ cup (½ stick/55 g) you need for the rolls.

DESSERTS

FREQUENTLY ASKED QUESTIONS

Hello, Bonnet Heads! This is your section. I actually set up an e-mail account at one point so that fans of the show could send in questions. I was pleasantly surprised—not just by the questions themselves, but also by the number of questions that I received. There are a lot of Bonnet Heads out there! I got questions from all over the United States and Canada and a few from France. Several of them were from as far away as Australia. So I boiled them down to the most frequently asked, and here they are. Thanks so much for helping me with this project—it was such fun!

1. *How did the real Laura inspire you in your acting and portrayal of her? Did you read all of the* Little House on the Prairie *books, her additional writings (published in the newspapers of her time), or do any research on your own? I am curious about your emotional connection to the real Laura.*
   —Rita from Pittsburgh, Pennsylvania

Laura is very similar to me. Based on the first two books, which I did read before we shot the pilot, I knew that I didn't have to create a character that was too different from my own personality. Remember, I was only nine years old, so I didn't really have a process for my performance yet. I was just so excited that I'd be able to dress up as Laura and live her adventures. It did get a little harder as Laura got older. The character eventually surpassed me in life experiences, so then I had to use my imagination and act the role. Until then, it was just instinct.

2. *When everyone sat down for dinner on* Little House on the Prairie, *what kind of food were you all really eating?*
   —Ann from Cary, North Carolina

As I said earlier, Kentucky Fried Chicken! We also ate Dinty Moore beef stew, Pillsbury biscuits, pies from the local grocery store, even peanut butter and jelly sandwiches. For the Olesons' house, there was roast beef, potatoes, green beans, roast potatoes, and gravy. Generally, the food came from the commissary at the studio where we were shooting. Whatever the food was, there were always leftovers, and the cast and crew would devour them!

3. *How did you get along with the child extras on the set?*
   —Erin from Calgary, Alberta

We all got along great. We played together on and off the set. There were no social lines drawn on our set. No one had a private trailer, not even Mike or Karen. We each had the exact same tiny cubicle to change in. No one got special treatment, which was a wonderful thing.

4. *Do you feel as if you did justice to Laura's character?*
   —Wendi from Fargo, North Dakota

Gosh, I sure hope so. I sure tried to.

5. *What* Little House *items that you took home from the set do you still have today?*
                                    —Gina from Coral Springs, Florida

I have Pa's fiddle, my script from the pilot, my red dress from the end credits, Victor French's hat and shirt and shoes, the Wilder's Room & Board sign, and the sheet music for the opening theme song written and signed by the composer, David Rose.

6. *How much input did Michael Landon have on your interpretation of Laura? Did he allow any freedom of character interpretation?*
                                    —Rona-Laurie from New York, New York

Mike allowed absolute freedom of interpretation. He respected all of our abilities as actors. Occasionally, he'd guide one of us through a particular scene, but I know he hired each of us because he appreciated the interpretations he saw in our screen tests.

7. *Other than Michael Landon, who was your favorite person on the set of* Little House on the Prairie? *And why?*
                                    —Ben from Lakewood, Colorado

Hands down, Alison Arngrim, who played Nellie Oleson. We got along from day one. She's the only cast member aside from Mike that I had a consistent relationship with off the set. We are still really close today. Mostly because she's smart and funny and kind and . . . and . . . and . . .

8. *Was there anything that Laura Ingalls did in real life or in the books that you wish you had been able to do on the show? Something that wasn't written in the story lines?*
                                    —Robin from Los Angeles, California

Maybe playing catch with a pig's bladder—although I'm not entirely sure I would have wished for that when I was a kid! Beyond that, I can't think of anything. In all seriousness, playing Laura really was like a big game of dress-up or make-believe for me. It was an adventure every day.

9. *As Half-Pint, you used to run out of the little house and across the prairie a lot. Did you actually like running that much, or was it just part of the job? You also went fishing a lot; did you like fishing as much?*
—Jennifer from Pennsylvania

Back then, running was no problem! Now, running is my least favorite way to get cardio. And I love fishing. Always have. I don't fish nearly as much now as I'd like to. There's just not enough time.

10. *Your first day on the set, you were so young. How was it? Were you scared out of your mind? Excited?*
—Ashley from Pensacola, Florida

Honestly, I was fearless. I don't think I knew enough to be scared. I was thrilled to go on location. I loved everything about it. Now I always get nervous on my first day of work, whatever the project. Back then, everything was just one big adventure to me.

11. *In one season your teeth were cute and crooked, but then in the next season they were beautiful and straight. How did that happen so quickly?*
—Kelley from Tarzana, California

Super braces! Actually, it was a long, slow process—much longer than it was for other kids. I had retainers and rubber bands and neck gear when we were filming. I had braces when we were on hiatus. Alison Arngrim had her braces the entire time, but she covered them with wax. Her teeth straightened much more quickly than mine did. Then again, Alison only had crooked teeth. I also had a wicked overbite!

12. *Did the cast have a favorite activity to do together while waiting to film?*
—Amanda from North Hollywood, California

We did lots of different things. We played cards, board games, Frisbee, and football. What stands out in my memory are the epic Ping-Pong games with cast and crew teams. The games were fierce, but fun. Michael Landon and Kent McCray dominated. Their team was called "The Jew and the Giant."

13. *What steps did you take to cry (with tears streaming down your face) for an emotional scene?*

—Megan from Rockford, Illinois

Honestly, it differed. Sometimes it was enough to imagine that I was in the same situation as Laura. Sometimes I'd cry because Michael or Karen was crying. Sometimes I'd think of something in my life that made me sad. Sometimes the makeup guys would put fake tears on my cheeks and that would be enough to make me cry for real. As much time as I spent running on the show, I think I spent ten times more than that crying.

14. *How much of farming life did you ever have to do or try to do on the show, such as milking cows, collecting eggs, helping plant a harvest, and so on?*

—Michelle from California (transplanted from Tennessee)

I've milked a cow, collected eggs, mucked stalls, and churned butter. I mean, I know how to do all of those things for a few minutes at a time as long as a prop man or wrangler is nearby. However, I can definitely bait my own hook!

15. *In many episodes of* Little House on the Prairie, *there is a certain actor who played several different roles. He has black hair and a mustache, and he can be seen as a church member, a stagecoach driver, and various other roles. Who is he?*

—Shelly from Hot Springs, Arkansas

I believe you are referring to Jack Lilley. He was also Victor French's photo and stunt double. Jack is a wrangler today. I have worked with him a couple of times since *Little House* ended. He remains a dear and true friend. I'm guessing Jack was in so many episodes because he was a good friend of Mike Landon's and because he was a very talented stuntman and actor.

16. *Will there ever be a* Little House on the Prairie *reunion show?*

—Lenoir from Wilkesboro, North Carolina

We have talked about it for years, but it would be very hard to do without Mike, Victor, Dabbs, Kevin, and all our other cast mates who have passed away.

Melissa Gilbert
% National Broadcasting Company
3000 W. Alameda
Burbank, California 91505

Dear Friend:

First, I want to thank you very much for your nice
letter. It was very thoughtful of you to take the
time to write to me and I hope you enjoy the "Little
House On The Prairie" shows as much as I enjoy making
them for you.

It's lots of fun working with Michael Landon and all
of the other people that work so hard to bring the
show into your home and we all hope that you will
continue to watch our series!

I'm ten years old and in the sixth grade at the school
I go to in Southern California. When we're filming, I
have school right on the set with the other children
that perform in the show.

My hobbies are dancing, music and collecting things
for my doll house. I also like art and drawing pictures
of landscapes and flowers. One of my favorite places
is the beach where I collect shells and rocks. Disney-
land and Magic Mountain are among my favorite places
too!

The colors I like best are Sky Blue, Navy Blue, Green,
Yellow and Orange.

My brother, Jonathan Gilbert, age 7, is also in the show
and he plays "Willie", the storekeeper's son and sometimes he's fun to work with too!

Thanks again for writing and may **your** life be full of
joy and happiness!

Sincerely,

Melissa Gilbert

Melissa Gilbert

WILDER'S
ROOM & BOARD

GOOD OLD RICE PUDDING

While we were filming *Little House* on our soundstages, I would have lunch at the commissary on the lot. They had the most amazing rice pudding. It was served in one of those fancy tall glass soda fountain dishes with whipped cream and a cherry on top. I even had to use a special long spoon to get to the bottom. Just thinking about that rice pudding makes me smile. Now that I make it myself, I usually skip the raisins.

Serves 4 to 6

1 quart (960 ml) milk
2 large eggs
½ cup (100 g) granulated sugar
½ cup (100 g) white rice
½ cup (75 g) raisins (optional)
1 tablespoon unsalted butter, melted
1 teaspoon vanilla extract
⅛ teaspoon ground nutmeg

- Preheat the oven to 300°F (150°C). Grease a 2-quart (2-L) baking dish.

- Beat together the milk and eggs in a large bowl. Stir in the sugar, rice, raisins (if using), butter, vanilla, and nutmeg.

- Pour the mixture into the prepared baking dish. Bake uncovered for 2 to 2½ hours, stirring frequently during the first hour. It's done when it's firm throughout and golden brown on top. Let the pudding rest for about 10 minutes before serving.

THE BEST
BANANA PUDDING

I don't know about you, but pudding for me is the cure for all that ails. It's great when you have a sore throat, or a toothache, or if you're just feeling a bit blue. Bananas are comforting and good for settling an upset tummy. So what could be better for us than banana pudding? The only answer I can find is: nothing! Nothing is better for us than banana pudding! Now, you may think I'm just trying to justify a reason to eat banana pudding. Here's the best reason ever: because it makes you happy, and isn't happiness what we are all looking for? I've sampled many banana puddings in my day, and I created this recipe as a tribute to all the banana puddings I've loved before.

continued

- Heat the milk in the top of a double boiler over medium heat.

- In a small bowl, whisk together ¾ cup (150 g) of the sugar, the cornstarch, egg yolks, and enough water to make a soupy paste (about ¼ cup/60 ml). Whisk the egg yolk mixture into the heated milk. Cook, stirring constantly, until thickened to the consistency of pudding, 30 to 40 minutes.

- Remove from the heat; stir in the vanilla. Let cool slightly.

- Preheat the oven to 350°F (175°C). Cover the bottom of a 9-by-13-inch (23-by-33-cm) baking dish with some of the vanilla wafers. Slice the bananas ½ inch (12 mm) thick and layer half of the slices over the cookies. Cover with half of the pudding. Add one more layer of cookies, bananas, and pudding.

- Put the egg whites in a bowl with the cream of tartar and beat until soft peaks form. Add the remaining 1 tablespoon sugar and continue to beat until stiff. Spread the meringue over the pudding and bake for 20 to 30 minutes, until lightly browned. Let it cool for about 10 minutes before serving.

1 quart (960 ml) milk
¾ cup plus 1 tablespoon (160 g) granulated sugar
¼ cup (30 g) cornstarch
4 large eggs, separated
4 teaspoons unsalted butter, softened
2 teaspoons vanilla extract
1 (12-ounce/340-g) box vanilla wafers
3 or 4 firm bananas
¼ teaspoon cream of tartar

MELISSA'S NUTLESS CARROT CAKE

Carrot cake is one of my very favorite things to make. I order it every time I'm in a restaurant that serves it, but I often find myself eating my way around the raisins and nuts! So I invented a raisin-free, nut-free recipe to suit my tastes. Now, if you want to add raisins and/or nuts, that's fine by me. Just don't expect me to join in any after-dinner conversation because I'll be busy picking them out of the cake!

Makes one 8-inch (20-cm) layer cake

For the Cake:

1 tablespoon unsalted butter, softened
1½ cups plus 2 tablespoons (185 g) all-purpose flour
1 cup (200 g) granulated sugar
1½ teaspoons baking soda
1 teaspoon baking powder
1 teaspoon ground cinnamon
½ teaspoon ground cloves
½ teaspoon ground nutmeg
½ teaspoon ground allspice
½ teaspoon salt
⅔ cup (165 ml) vegetable oil
3 large eggs, lightly beaten
1½ pounds (680 g) carrots, peeled and grated (about 4 cups)

For the Frosting:

12 ounces (340 g) cream cheese, softened
7 tablespoons (100 g) unsalted butter, softened
1 tablespoon vanilla extract
3 cups (300 g) confectioners' sugar, sifted

- Preheat the oven to 350°F (175°C). Grease two 8-inch (20-cm) round cake pans with the butter and dust each with 1 tablespoon of the flour, tapping out any excess.

- Make the cake: Combine the remaining 1½ cups (180 g) flour, the granulated sugar, baking soda, baking powder, cinnamon, cloves, nutmeg, allspice, and salt in a large bowl. Add the oil and eggs and blend until smooth. Add the carrots and mix well.

- Divide the batter between the prepared pans. Bake until a toothpick inserted in the center comes out clean, about 25 minutes. Let them cool on a rack, then remove the cakes from the pans.

- Make the frosting: Beat the cream cheese, butter, and vanilla in a mixing bowl with an electric mixer on high speed until smooth. Reduce the speed to low and beat in the confectioners' sugar.

- Put one cake round on a cake plate and spread one-third of the frosting on top. Set the second cake round on top and frost the sides and top of the cake with the remaining frosting.

TRIPLE STRAWBERRY CAKE

One day after work while I was on *Little House*, I went strawberry picking. I was so excited every time I found a strawberry that I ate it then and there. I ate every berry I picked. An hour later, when it was time to go, I went home empty handed but my fingertips were dyed red and I had a big berry-stain smile on my face.

continued

- Preheat the oven to 350°F (175°C). Grease and flour two 9-inch (23-cm) round cake pans.

- Make the cake: Whisk together the flour, baking powder, and salt in a medium bowl. Whisk together the milk and jam in a small bowl.

- In a large bowl, beat together the granulated sugar, oil, eggs, and vanilla with an electric mixer on medium-high speed until pale and smooth, 2 to 3 minutes. In three additions, alternately add the dry and wet ingredients to the sugar mixture, beginning and ending with the dry; mix until combined.

- Divide the batter between the prepared pans and smooth the tops; bake until a toothpick inserted in the middle of the cakes comes out clean, about 40 minutes. Let them cool for 15 minutes, then turn out onto a wire rack and cool completely.

- Make the frosting: In a large bowl, beat the butter and cream cheese with a mixer on high speed until smooth and fluffy, about 2 minutes. Add the confectioners' sugar and strawberry extract; beat until smooth.

- Place one cake round on a cake stand and spread one-third of the frosting on top. Cover with the second cake; frost the sides and top of the cake with the remaining frosting. Refrigerate the cake for 1 hour before serving.

- When ready to serve, hull and halve the strawberries and decorate the top with the strawberry halves. Let the cake sit at room temperature to take the chill off before serving.

For the Cake:

3 cups (375 g) all-purpose flour
1 tablespoon baking powder
½ teaspoon salt
1 cup (240 ml) milk
½ cup (160 g) seedless strawberry jam
2 cups (400 g) granulated sugar
1 cup (240 ml) canola oil
3 large eggs
1 teaspoon vanilla extract

For the Frosting:

1 cup (2 sticks/230 g) unsalted butter, softened
8 ounces (225 g) cream cheese, softened
1 (1-pound/455-g) box confectioners' sugar, sifted
1 teaspoon strawberry extract

1 cup (145 g) small strawberries, for decoration

SPICY SPICE CAKE

This is a lovely, aromatic cake for when the weather is cooler. I love warm spice flavors, and this cake has them all.

 *continued*

For the Cake:

2½ cups (285 g) cake flour
1 teaspoon baking powder
1 teaspoon baking soda
1 teaspoon salt
1 teaspoon ground cinnamon
½ teaspoon ground ginger
¼ teaspoon ground cloves
¼ teaspoon ground nutmeg
½ cup (1 stick/115 g) unsalted
    butter, softened
½ cup (110 g) firmly packed light
    brown sugar
1 cup (200 g) granulated sugar
2 large eggs
1 teaspoon vanilla extract
1¼ cups (300 ml) buttermilk

For the Frosting:

1½ cups (330 g) firmly packed
    light brown sugar
2 egg whites
1 tablespoon light corn syrup
1 teaspoon vanilla extract
½ teaspoon salt

- Preheat the oven to 350°F (175°C). Grease and flour two 8-inch (20-cm) round cake pans.

- Make the cake: Sift together the flour, baking powder, baking soda, salt, cinnamon, ginger, cloves, and nutmeg in a medium bowl.

- Beat the butter in a mixing bowl until creamy. Add the brown sugar, granulated sugar, eggs, and vanilla and beat using an electric mixer on high speed for 5 minutes, or until light and fluffy. Scrape down the sides of the bowl often. Add the sifted dry ingredients, alternating with the buttermilk, mixing on the lowest speed just until smooth.

- Pour the batter into the prepared pans and bake for 30 minutes, or until a wooden skewer or cake tester inserted in the center comes out clean. Cool in the pans on a wire rack for 5 minutes, then turn the cakes out of the pans onto the rack to cool completely.

- Make the frosting: Bring a pan of water to a boil. Combine the brown sugar, egg whites, syrup, vanilla, salt, and ⅓ cup (75 ml) cold water in a medium heatproof mixing bowl. Beat for 1 minute using an electric mixer on high speed. Place the bowl over the boiling water and cook, beating constantly for 7 minutes, until soft peaks form. Remove the bowl from the heat and continue beating with the mixer until a spreading consistency is reached.

- Put one cake round on a cake plate and spread one-third of the frosting on top. Set the second cake round on top and frost the sides and top of the cake with the remaining frosting.

PRAIRIE PEACH COBBLER

Talk about a perfect prairie dessert. You could use canned peaches for this, but it's just so much better with fresh peaches. Besides, I seriously doubt any Ingalls woman worth a hoot would use anything but fresh in-season peaches!

continued

- Preheat the oven to 350°F (175°C).

- Put the butter in a 9-by-13-inch (23-by-33-cm) baking dish and place it in the oven until the butter melts. Remove from the oven, tilt the dish to distribute the butter all over the bottom, and set aside.

- In a medium bowl, mix together 1 cup (200 g) of the sugar and the flour and stir in the milk. The batter will have a few lumps, but that's okay. Pour the batter on top of the melted butter.

- Put the peaches, the remaining 1 cup (200 g) of sugar, and 1 cup (240 ml) of water in a medium saucepan and bring to a boil, then reduce the heat and simmer for about 10 minutes.

- Spoon the fruit on top of the batter and then slowly pour the liquid from the saucepan on top of that. Be careful not to mix the fruit into the batter. Sprinkle with the cinnamon.

- Bake for 35 to 45 minutes, until bubbling and the top is golden. Serve warm.

½ cup (1 stick/115 g) unsalted butter
2 cups (400 g) granulated sugar
¾ cup (95 g) self-rising flour
¾ cup (180 ml) milk
2 cups (300 g) sliced fresh peaches
1 tablespoon ground cinnamon

BUTTER TARTS

You might have figured out by now that I'm not much of a raisin fan. Once while I was shooting a movie in Canada, my leading man invited me to dinner at his parents' house. The dinner was amazing, and my friend whispered in my ear, "Wait until dessert." Imagine my surprise when these gorgeous butter tarts came out. I cut into one, butter oozing everywhere, and then I saw them . . . the dreaded raisins. There was no way out, so I put a bite in my mouth, ready to act like it was the best dessert ever. Imagine my surprise when it turned out to be just that. To this day, these butter tarts are the only food I enjoy that contains raisins.

 Makes about 24 tarts

For the Tart Shells:

5½ cups (685 g) unbleached all-purpose flour
1½ teaspoons salt
1 pound (455 g) vegetable shortening, cold, cut into pieces
1 large egg
1 tablespoon white vinegar

For the Filling:

2 cups (290 g) raisins
2 cups (440 g) packed light brown sugar
½ cup (120 ml) maple syrup
¼ cup (60 ml) light corn syrup
3 tablespoons unsalted butter, cut into pieces
4 large eggs
1 teaspoon vanilla extract

- Make the tart shells: Sift together the flour and salt in a large mixing bowl. Use a pastry cutter or two knives to work the shortening into the flour until it resembles coarse meal.

- Whisk together the egg, vinegar, and 1 cup (240 ml) of water in a medium mixing bowl, then add the mixture to the flour mixture and stir with a fork until the dough just begins to hold together. Press the dough into a ball, then transfer it to a lightly floured surface. Give the dough several quick kneads with the heel of your hand to make it smooth, then shape it into a ball. Wrap the dough in plastic and refrigerate for 1 hour or overnight.

- Make the filling: Put the raisins in a medium saucepan, cover with cold water by 1 inch (2.5 cm), and bring them to a boil over high heat. Drain, then immediately transfer the raisins to a medium bowl and add the brown sugar, maple syrup, corn syrup, and butter; stir until the butter melts and the mixture is well combined. Set aside to cool for 3 to 4 minutes.

- Beat 1 of the eggs in a small bowl, then add it to the raisin mixture and mix well. Repeat with the remaining 3 eggs. Stir in the vanilla.

- Preheat the oven to 425°F (220°C).

- Roll the dough out on a lightly floured surface to a ¼ inch (6 mm) thickness. Use a 4-inch (10-cm) round cookie cutter to cut out about 24 rounds, gathering the dough scraps into a ball and rerolling as needed. Fit the rounds into standard-size muffin pans, then fill each about three-quarters full with the filling. (Stir the filling before filling the tarts.)

- Bake for 10 to 15 minutes, until the crusts are light golden and the filling is barely set. Let cool, then lift out the tarts with a knife.

CHESS PIE

Chess pie—it's so simple and down-home. Kind of like pecan pie, but without those nasty crunchy pecans. Just the gooey buttery goodness of what surrounds them. The cornmeal adds a bit of texture. This pie is really rich, and it tastes even better the next day, after spending a night hanging out in the fridge. Serve this with ice cream, whipped cream, or just plain.

Makes one 9-inch (23-cm) pie

- Preheat the oven to 350°F (175°C).

- Beat the eggs in a large bowl. Add the sugar, buttermilk, cornmeal, vinegar, and vanilla. Stir in the melted butter. Do not overbeat.

- Follow the package directions for preparing a single-crust pie in a 9-inch (23-cm) pie pan. Pour the filling into the unbaked pie shell. Bake for 1 hour, until the pie is firm and set and the crust is golden. Let it cool to room temperature before serving; or let it cool, then refrigerate and serve cold.

3 large eggs
1½ cups (300 g) granulated sugar
2 tablespoons buttermilk
1 tablespoon cornmeal
1 teaspoon white vinegar
1 teaspoon vanilla extract
¼ cup (½ stick/55 g) unsalted butter, melted
Refrigerated or frozen piecrust for a single-crust pie, or your favorite homemade piecrust

GINGERSNAP-PUMPKIN PIE

Did somebody say *ginger*? Count me in. No need to use homemade gingersnaps for this piecrust unless you really want to. This recipe is a snap (hee, hee)!

 Makes one 9-inch (23-cm) pie

¾ cup (65 g) gingersnap cookie crumbs
2 tablespoons granulated sugar
2½ tablespoons unsalted butter, melted
1½ cups (365 g) canned pumpkin puree (not pumpkin pie filling)
1 (12-ounce/340-g) can evaporated milk
¾ cup (165 g) packed light brown sugar
2 large eggs
1 tablespoon cornstarch
1 teaspoon ground cinnamon
1 teaspoon vanilla extract
¼ teaspoon ground nutmeg
¼ teaspoon salt

- Preheat the oven to 325°F (165°C).

- Combine the cookie crumbs, granulated sugar, and melted butter in a 9-inch (23-cm) pie pan, pressing it into the bottom and sides. Bake for 5 minutes. Let it cool completely.

- Combine the pumpkin, milk, brown sugar, eggs, cornstarch, cinnamon, vanilla, nutmeg, and salt in a large bowl. Whisk until combined. Pour the filling into the crust.

- Bake for 1 hour, or until the pie is firm and has turned slightly golden on top. Let it cool completely before serving.

MAMA MEG'S APPLE PIE

What would a prairie cookbook be without an apple pie recipe? Warm apple pie is one of the most comforting foods ever invented and a real homesteader dessert. Melt a little Cheddar cheese on top, Papa Harry (my grandpa) style. Or serve it à la mode. Or just devour it as it is. I'm sorry to admit, I'm not even going to attempt a homemade piecrust here. I have consistently and repeatedly tried and failed at piecrust. I don't know why. Perhaps I died in a horrible piecrust accident in a past life. Anyway, I really love the modern convenience of Pillsbury All Ready piecrusts from the grocery store. They're as close to homemade as I'll ever get . . . in this lifetime, anyway.

continued

2 large spicy apples, peeled, cored,
and sliced

3 large sweet apples, peeled,
cored, and sliced

Juice of ½ lemon

½ cup (110 g) packed dark brown
sugar

1 tablespoon all-purpose flour

1 teaspoon ground cinnamon

1 teaspoon vanilla extract

½ teaspoon salt

½ teaspoon ground nutmeg

Refrigerated or frozen piecrust
for a double-crust pie, or your
favorite homemade piecrust

1½ teaspoons unsalted butter

1 egg white, mixed with
1 tablespoon water

Granulated sugar

- Preheat the oven to 375°F (190°C).

- In a large bowl, mix the apples, lemon juice, brown sugar, flour, cinnamon, vanilla, salt, and nutmeg with your hands.

- Follow the package directions for preparing a double-crust pie in a 9-inch (23-cm) pie pan. Pour the apple mixture into the crust, scraping the bowl. Cut the butter into small pieces and sprinkle it over the filling before adding the top crust. Glaze the top crust with the egg white mixture. Sprinkle with granulated sugar. Bake for 15 minutes, then reduce the heat to 350°F (175°C) and bake for another 45 minutes or so, until the filling is bubbling and the top crust is golden. Let it cool for about 10 minutes before serving.

COWBOY COOKIES

Giddyup! I first had cowboy cookies at the home of my best friend, Sandy Peckinpah. Here's the thing about Cowboy Cookies: You make 'em for a bunch of really hungry cowboys and they'll eat 'em no matter what. So I played with my own recipe. Use this version as a jumping-off point, then add in your own fixin's. Maybe some M&Ms or crushed walnuts. Whatever ya got in yer pantry there, little Missy . . . or Mister . . . don't want to offend any chuck wagon chefs out there! *Yeeehaawww!*

Makes about 4 dozen cookies

- Preheat the oven to 350°F (175°C). Grease two baking sheets.

- Beat together the shortening, granulated sugar, and brown sugar in a large bowl. Add the peanut butter, eggs, and vanilla. Sift together the flour, baking soda, baking powder, and salt in a medium bowl; add to the creamed mixture. Add the oats, bran flakes, and chocolate chips; mix well.

- Drop by rounded 2-tablespoon measures onto the prepared baking sheets, placing them 1 inch (2.5 cm) apart. Bake for 9 to 12 minutes, until the edges turn brown but the centers still look chewy. Cool the cookies on the baking sheets for 5 minutes, then transfer them to wire racks to cool completely.

2¼ cups (450 g) vegetable shortening
2 cups (400 g) granulated sugar
2½ (550 g) cups packed light brown sugar
¾ cup (190 g) chunky peanut butter
5 large eggs
2 teaspoons vanilla extract
4½ cups (560 g) all-purpose flour
2 teaspoons baking soda
1 teaspoon baking powder
1 teaspoon salt
3 cups (465 g) rolled oats
2½ cups (75 g) bran flakes
2 cups (335 g) semisweet chocolate chips

OLD-FASHIONED MOLASSES COOKIES

We ate a lot of molasses cookies on *Little House*. You know—the great big store-bought kind with the grains of sugar on top! The flavor of molasses cookies brings back wonderful memories for me, so I created this recipe. If you can't find whole-wheat pastry flour, increase the all-purpose flour to 1¾ cups (220 g) and use ¼ cup (30 g) regular whole-wheat flour.

Makes 32 cookies

½ cup (120 ml) unsweetened applesauce
1¼ cups (250 g) granulated sugar
6 tablespoons (85 g) butter, softened
¼ cup (60 ml) dark molasses
1 large egg
1 cup (125 g) all-purpose flour
1 cup (115 g) whole-wheat pastry flour
2 teaspoons baking soda
1 teaspoon ground cinnamon
½ teaspoon ground ginger
½ teaspoon ground cloves
½ teaspoon salt
Cooking spray

- Spoon the applesauce onto several layers of heavy-duty paper towels, spread out to a ½-inch (12-mm) thickness. Cover with additional paper towels and let it stand for 5 minutes. Scrape the sauce into a large bowl using a rubber spatula.

- Add 1 cup (200 g) of the sugar and the butter to the bowl and beat with an electric mixer on medium speed until well blended, about 3 minutes. Add the molasses and egg and beat well to combine.

- Combine the flours, baking soda, cinnamon, ginger, cloves, and salt in a medium bowl, stirring well with a whisk. Gradually add the flour mixture to the sugar mixture, beating until blended. Cover and freeze the dough for 30 minutes, or until firm.

- Preheat the oven to 375°F (190°C). Coat two baking sheets with cooking spray.

- With moist hands, shape the dough into thirty-two 1-inch (2.5-cm) balls. Roll the balls in the remaining ¼ cup (50 g) of sugar. Place them 3 inches (7.5 cm) apart on the baking sheets.

- Bake for 8 to 10 minutes. Cool on the baking sheets for 5 minutes, then transfer the cookies to wire racks to cool completely.

MY OATMEAL COOKIES

I'm a big fan of the oatmeal cookie, but, as I have stated in this book repeatedly, I have a deep aversion to raisins and nuts in my food. You might even say I'm raisin-and-nut-o-phobic. So I always leave out the raisins and nuts when I make these. You can add them in if you'd like. Just don't tell me about it.

 Makes about 2 dozen cookies

1 cup (2 sticks/230 g) unsalted butter, softened
1 cup (200 g) granulated sugar
1 cup (220 g) packed light brown sugar
2 large eggs
1 teaspoon vanilla extract
2 cups (250 g) all-purpose flour
1½ teaspoons ground cinnamon
1 teaspoon baking soda
1 teaspoon salt
3 cups (240 g) quick-cooking oats
1 cup (240 ml) raisins and/or chopped nuts of your choice (optional)

- In a large bowl, beat together the butter, granulated sugar, and brown sugar. Beat in the eggs one at a time, then stir in the vanilla.

- Combine the flour, cinnamon, baking soda, and salt in a medium bowl. Stir the dry ingredients into the creamed mixture. Mix in the oats. If you are using raisins and/or nuts (if using), mix them into the dough now, combining well. Cover and chill the dough for at least 1 hour.

- Preheat the oven to 375°F (190°C). Grease two baking sheets. Roll the dough into 1-inch (2.5-cm) balls and place them 2 inches (5 cm) apart on the baking sheets.

- Bake for 8 to 10 minutes, until light golden brown. Cool the cookies on the baking sheets for 5 minutes, then transfer them to wire racks to cool completely.

MELISSA ELLEN'S GINGER-MELON GINGERSNAPS

I am a ginger—I have a ginger melon!—and I love ginger! Gingersnaps, gingerbread, ginger candy, ginger ale, Ginger the castaway, my ginger husband (another melon!). Ginger beer, pickled ginger, crystallized ginger, ginger chews, minced ginger, ginger tea, ginger syrup, ginger perfume, ginger, ginger, *ginger*!

Did I mention that I love ginger?

Makes 6 dozen cookies

- Beat the brown sugar and butter in a large bowl using an electric mixer until smooth. Add the egg, fresh ginger, and lemon zest and beat well.

- In a separate large bowl, whisk together the flour, ground ginger, cinnamon, pepper, cloves, and baking powder. Gradually add the dry ingredients to the sugar-butter mixture, beating with the mixer until well combined. Form the dough into a large disk, wrap it in plastic, and chill for at least 4 hours or overnight.

- Preheat the oven to 350°F (175°C).

- Scoop out the dough in 1-teaspoon portions, roll into balls, and place them 2 inches (5 cm) apart on ungreased baking sheets. Press down hard with the base of a drinking glass dipped in flour to make thin rounds. Sprinkle the tops of the cookies with the raw sugar and bake for 8 to 10 minutes, until crisp and golden brown. Transfer the gingersnaps to wire racks to cool.

1¾ cups (385 g) firmly packed dark brown sugar

1½ cups (3 sticks/340 g) unsalted butter, softened

1 large egg

1 tablespoon grated peeled fresh ginger

½ teaspoon grated lemon zest

3¾ cups (465 g) all-purpose flour

2 tablespoons ground ginger

1 tablespoon ground cinnamon

½ teaspoon freshly ground white pepper

¼ teaspoon ground cloves

¼ teaspoon baking powder

2 tablespoons raw sugar

AFTER LITTLE HOUSE

After *Little House* ended its nine-year run, it was time for me to spread my wings as an actor and a person. While most kids were going to college, I was meeting with my manager and agents to plan the future of my career. It was very important stuff, but none of it was as important as having the chance to really say good-bye to the cast and crew during the final weeks of the show. It was a time of tremendous grief. Those final days saw all of us—cast, crew, everyone—bursting into tears and spontaneous embraces.

At that point, I was nineteen and had spent nearly half my life on that *Little House* set. I spent more time there than I had in my own home. Don't get me wrong—my family life was of great importance. It molded me into the woman I am today. But in many ways, I feel that my *Little House* family molded me even more. Not a day goes by that I don't reminisce about those times. My home is filled with *Little House* memorabilia. And my memory is long.

Even more than the tangible remnants of the show, the intangible remnants remain with me. When I direct, I direct like Mike Landon and Victor French. When I produce, it's much in the same way Kent McCray did. My posture is like Karen Grassle's. When I research a new role, I can hear Scottie MacGregor in my head, guiding me through my acting process. Dean's charm. Matthew's and Patrick's courage and humor. The Greenbush twins' sweetness. Alison's dear friendship! All of these things live on in me and, as a consequence, live on in my children and, hopefully, in theirs, and so on and so on. . . .

Little House on the Prairie will never truly end because it lives on in each of us who experienced it, whether you worked on the show or watched it on television.

It's impossible for me to tell where Half-Pint ends and Melissa begins. That is the real blessing for me. I had the chance to live out every little girl's fantasy, mine included. And I got to do that surrounded by the loving arms of my *Prairie* family. I truly am the luckiest girl in the world.

MY NEW
FRONTIER

My love

My children

ACKNOWLEDGMENTS

My very first thank-you goes out to my childhood friend Collette Wolas. When we were about eight years old, she taught me how to make scrambled eggs—delicious scrambled eggs with a little bit of garlic powder in them.

Next, I must thank my sweet mother, for whom I made the eggs the following Mother's Day. As I was making them, I figured, if a little garlic powder was good, then a half a bottle would be even better. Bless her heart. She ate the eggs, every last bite, telling me how delicious they were. My first rave review as a chef!

Next I must thank my grandfather, Harry Crane, for eating and enjoying my first experimental quesadillas. He loved them, and that helped to build my confidence as a cook even more.

To my beloved husband and children, who inspire me to create sumptuous meals for them. There are no accolades as meaningful as you around the table, loving what I've cooked. As I fill your tummies, you fill my heart. Forever love, my family . . . forever love.

To my best friend, Sandy Peckinpah. My soul sister. The best chef I've ever known, bar none. Cooking with you all these years has been a joy and an inspiration. Your friendship is my safe place. You truly are a blessing to all around you. And yes, I promise to let you teach me your brilliant piecrust. I think it's about time, don't you?

To Jennifer Levesque, Valerie Cimino, Holly Dolce, Sarah Massey, and everyone who was and is at Abrams. You all worked so hard and so long to help make my vision of the book a reality. And what fun we all had in the process! Thank you, thank you, thank you.

Karen Schaupeter, Dane Holweger, Chris Nowling, Kevin Scott, and Lauren Machen, who prepared my recipes and photographed them, me, and my family so beautifully. Those three days we worked together were such fun and so yummy!

Vivian Turner, thank you, as always, for dressing me impeccably for that shoot. Hard to believe that we've been working together for nearly three decades, since we are still only in our twenties! I love you, sweet Viv!

Amanda Benzaken, thank you for your extraordinary job with my hair and makeup. You made me feel beautiful that day.

To my literary agent, Dan Strone. I am so grateful to have you involved in my career as a writer. Your guidance and enthusiasm for my ideas are always greatly appreciated.

I owe a long-standing debt of gratitude to my publicists, Ame Van Iden and Janet Ringwood at PMK*BNC. Thanks lady-faces . . . not only for working so hard but for all the years of friendship, protection, support, loyalty, and laughter.

Marc Schwartz, your unwavering enthusiasm and support though the course of this project will not be forgotten.

To my amazing friends, who have shared so much with me. Some of my very favorite times have been when we all get together and cook huge, sumptuous meals. I love you all so much.

To the dear fans of *Little House on the Prairie*. It has been my honor to spend all of these years with you. Thank you for your love, loyalty, and support.

And finally, I must thank my "Prairie" family: Mike, Karen, Kent, Sue, Victor, Maury, Hank, Uncle Miles, Alison, Rachel, Jack, Ron H., Ron C., I. W., Jerry, Richalene, Linda, Whitey, Teddy, Larry, C. T., Gladys, Lonny, Mrs. Minniear, Mrs. Fife, Matt, Frank, Pat, Brian, Kyle, Ruthy, Dean B., Dean W., Hersha, Charlotte S., Charlotte R-Y., Mary, Kenny, Erika, Radames, Lillian, Vince, Steve, Brad, David, Paula, Mike M., Mike T., Burkey, Lucy-Lee, Andy, Buzzy, Scottie, Bill C., Bill S., Stan, Reid, Glen, Richard, Bear, Dick, Merlin, Dallas, Pamela, Karl, Linwood, Deb, Kevin, Dabbs, Ketty, Dub, Brenda, Wendy, Lindsay K., Leslie, Mike Jr., Brianne, Marvin, Jason, Matt J., Melissa F., Allison B., Luke, Robin . . . and the list goes on and on. Please forgive me if there are names missing. It's not that I've forgotten any of them; it's just that if I wrote them all, this book would be as long as *War and Peace*.

You people raised me. Taught me so much of what I know professionally and personally. Your love for me was and is palpable. Each of you left an indelible mark on my heart.

I love you all so much and will always, always be . . .

Your Half-Pint

INDEX